Research
Universities

And the Challenges of Globalization: An International Convocation

Proceedings from the Centennial Meeting
of the Association of American Universities
April 22–23, 2001
Washington, D.C.

The Association of American Universities (AAU) is an organization of sixty-three leading public and private research universities in the United States and Canada. (AAU membership rose from sixty-one to sixty-three in April 2001, when Texas A&M University and Stony Brook University–State University of New York became members.)

The association was founded in 1900 by a group of fourteen Ph.D.-granting universities in the United States to strengthen and standardize U.S. doctoral programs.

Those goals have been accomplished. Today, the primary purpose of AAU is to provide a forum for the development and implementation of institutional and national policies promoting strong programs in academic research and scholarship, and in undergraduate, graduate, and professional education.

Library of Congress Cataloging-in-Publication Data
LOC Control Number: 2001095330
ISBN: 0-9704478-2-5

Available from:
Association of American Universities
1200 New York Avenue, NW, Suite 550
Washington, D.C. 20005
202/408-7500
Fax 202/408-8184

Ann Leigh Speicher, Editor
Design and production by Fletcher Design, Washington, D.C.
Copy editing by Steven B. Kennedy

CONTENTS

4

COMPETING DEMANDS ON UNIVERSITIES

5

THE IMPACT OF INFORMATION TECHNOLOGY ON UNIVERSITIES

6

TRENDS IN INTERNATIONAL UNIVERSITY COLLABORATION

7

SUMMARY AND IMPLICATIONS

8

THE VIEW FROM THE U.S. DEPARTMENT OF STATE

9

APPENDIXES

THE ROLE OF UNIVERSITIES IN MEETING THE CHALLENGES OF GLOBALIZATION

Nils Hasselmo
PRESIDENT, ASSOCIATION OF AMERICAN UNIVERSITIES

These proceedings are from the third and final meeting called to celebrate the centennial of the Association of American Universities, referred to often in this volume by its familiar acronym, AAU.

The first meeting, in April 2000, looked at the nature of research universities in North America, focusing particularly on their relations with business and government. The second was held in October 2000 at the University of Chicago, where AAU was founded in 1900. That meeting explored the future of research and scholarship within the university, with a focus on the core disciplines of the biological sciences, the physical sciences and engineering, the social sciences, and the humanities.

For the third centennial meeting in April 2001 it seemed most appropriate to look beyond North America to the role of research universities in helping people around the world deal with the economic and cultural opportunities—and the challenges—of globalization and information technology.

Although universities from every region face their own special issues and challenges, our program committee believed that all universities were grappling with similar difficulties related to the globalization of information, the exploding demand for postsecondary education, and the need to promote economic development through scholarship and research.

We were interested in how different institutions were balancing the multitude of demands on today's universities, and how they were collaborating to help their nations and regions adapt to globalization. We felt sure that despite the differing circumstances of research universities around the world, we would find much common ground.

During our meeting in Washington, D.C., university leaders from six continents came together to share their approaches to these issues and to explore opportunities for further cooperation. I wish to express my deepest appreciation to all of our international guests and to our own AAU presidents and chancellors for making the international convocation a success. I also extend my sincere thanks to our master of ceremonies, AAU chairman **Charles Vest**, to program committee chairman **Malcolm Gillis** and his colleagues on that committee, and to the AAU staff for their work in shaping the program.

It was clear from our discussions that for a host of economic and cultural reasons, universities are a vital resource for their nations and regions. While helping their societies meet the economic and employment challenges of globalization, they also are preserving culture and traditions.

Universities everywhere are facing the twin challenges of rapid technological change and multiple demands on their resources, but those in the developing world have added burdens—dwindling resources, exploding numbers of potential students, competition from private sector providers, brain drain, and political interference.

Speakers and participants agreed that along with expanded regional and bilateral collaborations, postsecondary institutions in the developing world must have greater access to electronic teaching and research materials, including scholarly journals. But it was also clear from our discussions that universities throughout the world have much to learn from one another, not only through research and scholarly projects, but also through the exchange of students and faculty. The benefits are mutual.

Our conversations were rich and thought-provoking. It is our hope that the ideas presented here will enhance mutual understanding and lead to collaborative action.

In the opening session, "Globalization, Economic Development, and Cultural Identity: Forces and Counterforces," Harvard University professor emeritus **Henry Rosovsky**, co-chairman of a World Bank/UNESCO study on higher education in developing countries, laid out the long odds facing universities in developing nations. He noted that whereas 85 percent of the world's population lives in developing nations, those countries account for fewer than half of the world's college students. But higher education is more important than ever to developing nations because of its role in transforming knowledge into economic wealth, preserving culture, and educating a nation's leaders.

In the same session, we also heard from two of our international guests. **Zhihong Xu**, president of Peking University, reported on how China is using its universities to help the nation integrate into the broader international economy. Universities are expanding enrollments, gaining greater access to telecommunications technologies, increasing the diversity of their courses, and developing new international collaborations.

Luis Alfredo Riveros, rector of the University of Chile, focused on the importance of universities as the "think tanks" of their nations—institutions able to bring a variety of resources and perspectives to solving problems—and as the repositories and protectors of the nation's culture. Because many of those tasks would not be met through market forces, he argued, governments must continue to finance their universities and not abandon them to uncertain support from the private sector.

In a separate presentation that evening, **His Highness the Aga Khan**, hereditary Imam of the Shia Imami Ismaili Muslims, reemphasized the importance of higher education in the developing world, where it operates under enormous pressures. Using the examples of the Aga Khan University in Pakistan and the new University of Central Asia, both founded through his efforts, he noted how private institutions can serve as valuable role models for universities and other institutions in developing nations. Private universities not only can provide high-quality academic programs, but also enlightened policies in admissions, financial aid, and university governance.

In addition, they can set an important example by focusing their research efforts on the social and economic needs of their societies and sharing their experience and human resources with other institutions.

The competing demands on contemporary universities were the topic of the first session on the next day. Berkeley chancellor **Robert Berdahl** led off by noting that few institutions had as many stakeholders as universities—faculty, students, parents, business and industry, government, and the public—each with its own, often conflicting, set of requirements. Moreover, the information revolution and globalization are creating a new set of demands on universities. As a result of these multiple obligations, he said, every university faces resource limitations that require difficult choices.

Sir Alec Broers of the University of Cambridge stressed that it was most important for universities to put into place academic and administrative structures that will allow them to adapt rapidly to and take best advantage of the information and communications revolutions. Especially in developed nations, universities struggle to find the resources necessary to attract and retain high-quality faculty and students, said Broers. Moreover, the balances between general education and specialization—and between the expensive needs of science and technology and sustenance of the arts and humanities—are always difficult.

Juan Ramón de la Fuente, rector of the National Autonomous University of Mexico, focused on the fact that although many trade barriers have been lowered in North America, significant obstacles still impede the flow of technical personnel across borders. He also stressed the importance of today's university students having not just technical expertise, but also "intercultural competence"—the ability to work well on multicultural teams, speak other languages, and deal effectively with diversity.

Shigehiko Hasumi, president emeritus of the University of Tokyo, focused on the historical development of universities in Japan as part of the nation's infrastructure, and on how his country's universities now need to broaden their thinking and eliminate discrimination based on gender, age, and nationality.

Introducing the session on the impact of information technology on universities, **Alan Gilbert**, vice-chancellor of the University of Melbourne, maintained that the world could not meet the growing demand for higher education with traditional, campus-based universities. Thirty million people in the world today are fully qualified to attend a university but can find no place, he said. That number will rise to 100 million people in the next decade. Such needs can only be met, Gilbert asserted, through new communications technologies.

Focusing on the challenges that information technologies pose to universities, former University of Michigan president **James Duderstadt** expressed the expectation that the evolution of digital technologies would continue at an exponential pace in the foreseeable future, with "rapid, profound, and unpredictable change" leading perhaps to a restructuring of the higher education enterprise into a global knowledge and learning industry.

While acknowledging the rapid pace of technological change, Duke University president **Nan Keohane** expressed optimism that the institution of the university would survive the digital age. Universities are resilient, she said, and many of their elements, such as undergraduate residential education and the path to the doctoral degree, will endure because they are valuable and widely valued. She expressed the expectation that the best education one day would be delivered both in geographic space and in cyberspace.

Collaborations are important in helping universities deal with tight resources and rapid change. Rice University president Malcolm Gillis, in his introduction to the session on international collaborations, noted a renewed interest among AAU universities in a wide array of international programs— from formal associations like the Association of Pacific Rim Universities to bilateral programs for business education and management.

Peter Gaehtgens, president of the Free University of Berlin, discussed how nations in the European Union are working to harmonize their higher education systems. That is proving difficult, he said, because educational systems are quite different, and the principles they represent are part of each nation's cultural identity. While large, institutionalized networks of schools are trying to harmonize higher education, he said, smaller groups and strategic alliances of similar universities are enabling universities to develop well-integrated research and teaching programs.

Peter McPherson, president of Michigan State University and former administrator of the U.S. Agency for International Development, stressed the importance of collaborations between universities in the developed and developing worlds, particularly in agriculture. Along with direct collabora-tions, he said, universities in the industrialized world must work with gov-ernment agencies and others to make scholarly publications available to the developing countries on the Internet. He congratulated the Massachusetts Institute of Technology for its announced intention to place courseware on the Internet so that teachers could use and adapt it freely.

In summing up the program, **George Rupp**, president of Columbia University, focused on the pushes and pulls on the university from what he called the monastic and scholastic impulses. The monastic impulse, said Rupp, centers on liberal education and curiosity-driven research. The scholastic impulse, by contrast, is responsive to social challenges, employers seeking skilled employees, and government efforts to promote economic growth. Universities must continue to serve their societies in a host of ways, in Rupp's view, but "we must also remain faithful to our core purposes of liberal education and pure scholarship—curiosity-driven research." Through this role, he said, we resist "the attempt to domesticate the university com-pletely to its secular, utilitarian purposes."

Bernard Shapiro, principal of McGill University, agreed that the meet-ing demonstrated the difficult balancing act universities face between coop-eration and competition, and between global thinking and the need to preserve national culture and identity. He added that what was appropriate for a university in one nation might not be appropriate in another. He also saw irony in the oft-repeated statement that the greater availability of infor-mation would make institutions less important and individuals more impor-tant. The reverse may be true. "Access to information is not the same as the capacity to deal with information in a productive way," he said. "It is how we turn information into knowledge that is critical."

That evening, at a reception and dinner at the U.S. State Department, Secretary of State **Colin Powell** told the university leaders that their activities were vital to the world's future. Not only will many of the challenges facing the world require the basic knowledge created in universities, he said, but universities are "educating tomorrow's leaders—the leaders who will even-tually build the peaceful and prosperous world that we all look forward to."

In spite of the many difficulties identified, the underlying tone of AAU's international convocation echoed Secretary Powell's note of cautious optimism.

1

WELCOMING REMARKS

Charles M. Vest

PRESIDENT, MASSACHUSETTS INSTITUTE OF TECHNOLOGY

G ood afternoon. It is a great pleasure to welcome you to this opening session of our meeting. It is an extraordinary privilege for me to serve as chairman of the Association of American Universities (AAU) on the occasion of its centennial.

AAU members know that this convocation is the culmination of a year-long celebration of our 100th year of existence. We began the celebration a year ago here in Washington with a discussion of the future of our universities from the perspective of their growing partnerships with government and industry. Our discussion continued last fall at the University of Chicago, where we thought together about the future of the academic disciplines. It concludes today as we consider the international context of our institutions and of higher education. Together we will ponder the role of research universities in helping people around the world take advantage of the economic and cultural opportunities offered by globalization and information technology.

We are delighted to have fifty leaders of universities from six continents join us in this celebration. Their presence makes this a remarkable meeting.

On behalf of the presidents and chancellors of AAU, I welcome all of you and thank you for your presence and participation.

2

GLOBALIZATION, ECONOMIC DEVELOPMENT, AND CULTURAL IDENTITY: FORCES AND COUNTERFORCES

APRIL 22, 2001

Our purpose in this session is to explore the role of higher education in developing national and global economies. We are particularly pleased to have three colleagues—one each from Chile, China, and the United States—join us in thinking about these matters.

Last year the World Bank and the United Nations Educational, Scientific, and Cultural Organization (UNESCO) convened a task force on higher education in developing countries. The co-chairman of that task force, Professor Henry Rosovsky, university professor emeritus at Harvard University, will open this session. Professor Rosovsky's remarks will be followed by regional perspectives from Zhihong Xu, president of Peking University, and Luis Alfredo Riveros, rector of the University of Chile.

Henry Rosovsky is the Louis P. and Linda L. Geyser University Professor Emeritus at Harvard. He is a scholar of great accomplishments in the fields of economics and history, particularly Japanese economic history. After beginning his teaching career at the University of California, Berkeley, he moved to Harvard University in 1965. At Harvard he served as chairman of the economics department, dean of the faculty of arts and sciences, and twice as acting president. He has received fifteen honorary degrees from institutions around the world, including the Hebrew University of Jerusalem and Harvard University.

When I first came to Cambridge ten years ago someone said to me, "The real advantage of living here is that you can be a neighbor and friend of Henry Rosovsky." That's true.

—Charles M. Vest
President, Massachusetts
Institute of Technology

Responsibilities and Challenges of Higher Education in the Developing World

Henry Rosovsky
Professor Emeritus, Harvard University

T hank you, Chuck, for that wonderful introduction. I find myself in a most unnatural position. Many years ago, Harvard's president, James Bryant Conant, was asked to supply the proper collective noun for deans. He suggested a "gripe" of deans.

That will tell you something about my normal relationship with the kinds of people—nearly all university presidents—sitting in this audience. I'm not able to gripe today, but I will express some opinions that you may interpret as gripes.

Many of you know that I am a walk-on. Malcolm Gillis of Rice University, a friend to whom I can never say no, invited me to appear before you because the person who was supposed to address you—Mamphela Ramphele, who co-chaired with me the report for the World Bank and UNESCO, *Higher Education in Developing Countries: Peril and Promise*— was not able to be here. I would like to talk about what we learned during that exercise.

The most accurate title for my remarks would be, "The Condition of Higher Education for 85 Percent of the World's Population." It is not a small topic—though that 85 percent provides fewer than half of the world's post-secondary students, a disproportion that is one of the problems facing the developing world. (We all recognize that in some cases "developing" is a euphemism.)

Higher education has never been more important than it is at this moment, but neither developing countries nor donor agencies have grasped that importance.

Among the reasons that compelled us to undertake the assignment we were offered was the opportunity to clarify some fundamental misperceptions about higher education—both within the developing countries and within donor agencies. Those misperceptions come, first, from inadequate techniques for evaluating the role of higher education in the past and, second, from a lack of clarity about its future in the developing world.

To cut immediately to the most important conclusion, higher education has never been more important than it is at this moment, but neither developing countries nor donor agencies have grasped that importance.

In pursuing our task, we framed three questions:
- What is the role of higher education in economic and social development?
- What are the major obstacles to its performing that role?
- What can be done to overcome those obstacles?

We attempted to answer our questions by examining five separate topics. The first relates to the public interest in higher education. The key finding here is that market forces will not deliver all that is necessary for higher education. I'll come back to that point.

The second topic pertains to systems of higher education. A rational national system is a necessary condition for higher education to perform its role in developing countries.

Third, as far as we could tell, there is nearly complete agreement in the developing world that prevailing governance practices and customs are a key obstacle—perhaps the key obstacle—to improving the quality of higher education.

Fourth, in the critical area of science and technology, the north-south gap is large and growing. It will not be closed in the near future, but perhaps we can stop it from widening.

And finally, general—or liberal—education is needed in the developing world. It is not a luxury, especially for future leaders in developing countries.

Before going into more detail about our three questions and five topics, let me describe the current situation by making some broad generalizations that apply on average to the developing world. I am not talking about any one country or even one group of countries.

The situation has two components: persistent problems dating from World War II and some significant new realities that have compounded those problems.

The long-standing problems are well known. The professoriate is often poorly trained. In many countries, few members of the faculty have advanced degrees. Pay is often pitiful, leading to excessive moonlighting. I have seen countries where a tape recorder supplies the lecture while the professor is at a second or third job trying to make enough money to put food on the table. I am not saying this to be critical; I'm just describing a reality.

In much of the developing world, learning is purely by rote. The professor gives a lecture; the students copy it down. Textbooks are inadequate. There is virtually no interaction in the classroom.

In many parts of the developing world, corruption and politicization affect the selection of faculty and administrators. I don't say that lightly. We looked into this quite carefully, and our report cites many examples.

I have seen countries where a tape recorder supplies the lecture while the professor is at a second or third job trying to make enough money to put food on the table.

In East Africa, Pakistan, and elsewhere, higher education has declined since the end of colonial rule. I do not wish to romanticize the colonial heritage, but the decline in some countries is a fact.

In a paper by Robert Edwards, the former president of Bowdoin College, I ran across a passage written by an Indian scholar about the University of Calcutta in 1917. He described the university as "altogether a foreign plant, imported into this country." While India had been enriched by Western education, the critic added, "there has been a cost, a cost as regards culture, a cost as regards respect for self and reverence for others, a cost as regards the nobility and dignity of life."

That is a very important passage, especially in view of your interest in taking culture into account—something we do only too rarely.

Eric Ashby, that well-known student of higher education, also noted declining standards. "Poverty," he observed, "by giving an unnatural momentum to the university system and so diluting the quality of its staff and students, was a major cause of the disastrous fall in standards." He said this about India many years ago. It is not true there today, but it remains true for many other countries.

The problems are mirrored in student travails. Facilities are inadequate. Students are often unprepared, and no remedial education is available. In several countries, students have a history of striking at exam time. Knowing they cannot pass the examinations, they go on strike in order to stay in school. That is probably better than unemployment.

As if the long-standing problems of insufficient resources and poor management were not enough, new realities are making the situation even more dire. The first of the new realities is the tremendous expansion of higher education in the developing world. The second is the consequence of that expansion, which I call "uncontrolled differentiation." The third, and perhaps most fundamental, is the knowledge revolution through which we are now living.

> The public sector has been the traditional source of higher education, but it cannot possibly cope with the increases in demand.

Over the past fifty years, the developing world has significantly expanded primary and secondary education. Even in sub-Saharan Africa, literacy has reached 50 percent, and it generally is higher elsewhere. The higher percentage of secondary school graduates, coupled with rapidly growing populations and a premium on greater skills, has created tremendous pressures on higher education in the developing world.

Everywhere in the developing world enrollments are rising more rapidly than population. Between 1975 and 1990, the number of people with some higher education increased by 250 percent.

In these countries, the public sector has been the traditional source of higher education, but it cannot possibly cope with the increases in demand. One of the consequences is mega-universities like the National University of Mexico and the University of Buenos Aires, each of which has more than 200,000 students. Another consequence is the major imbalance in access between urban and rural residents, the rich and the poor, men and women, and ethnic groups.

The increasing percentage of secondary school graduates, plus demographic trends, people's rising economic hopes, and the inability of the public sector to cope have resulted in what our report calls "unbridled, unplanned, and chaotic differentiation" among institutions.

Since the 1980s, private, for-profit higher education has been the most rapidly growing sector of tertiary education in the world. China has 800 private postsecondary institutions. Sixty percent of higher education in Brazil is private. Indonesia has 57 public institutions—and 1,200 private. An associated expansion has occurred in distance learning. Anadolu University in Turkey has 578,000 students. China TV University has 530,000 students.

These new pressures, piled on old problems, have created inescapable declines in quality. The private, for-profits don't resemble Stanford—or even the University of Phoenix. Many are of poor quality.

And now comes the final blow: the knowledge revolution. Recently I ran across a paragraph written by Jim Duderstadt, former president of the University of Michigan:

> Our world is in the midst of a social transition into a post-industrial society as our economies shift from material- and labor-intensive products and processes to knowledge-intensive products and services. A radically new system for creating wealth has evolved that depends upon the creation and application of new knowledge. We are in a transition period where intellectual capital, brainpower, is replacing financial and physical capital as the key to our strength, prosperity, and well being. In a very real sense, we are entering a new age, an age of knowledge in which the key strategic resource necessary for prosperity has become knowledge itself—that is, educated people and their ideas.

That is almost a cliché today, but it is rarely mentioned in the context of poor countries.

The current knowledge revolution comprises computerization, information technology, biomedical sciences, and more. Not surprisingly, it is the product of the advanced countries. Unlike earlier industrial revolutions, it is closely tied to higher education as a producer and consumer of its benefits.

Compare the leading edges of technology today with steam engines, iron and steel, traditional factories, and railroads. In those earlier examples, the role of science was attenuated. Practical concerns led scientific inquiry. Science did not begin to lead until just before World War II.

The change has made higher education immensely important. Research and education in universities are crucial to the advancement of our economies and our daily life. The emphasis today is on highly skilled human capital and much less on physical capital. Simple literacy and numeracy, provided by primary and secondary education, are no longer sufficient.

The knowledge revolution has further widened the gap between the developing world and the industrial economies. Closing that gap is hard to conceive, and even preventing further widening will be an extremely daunting task. But the developing world needs better higher education if it is to share in the benefits of the global economy.

I would like now to turn briefly to the five topics I previously mentioned. Let me begin with the issue of the public interest.

Social scientists are prone to measure the benefits of education in terms of its private returns—education gives us higher incomes and better lives. The social returns are usually defined in terms of the additional tax revenues that accrue from higher education. Thus my own material gains and tax payments measure the private and social returns of education. That is a very narrow view.

Private markets will not deliver all that is needed in higher education. They will not provide instruction and research in the humanities or the basic sciences, because there is no money to be made in either.

When these notions are combined with globalization, the "American model" of competition, and desires for economy and efficiency, policymakers in poorer parts of the world increasingly may be tempted to rely on market forces. If higher education is really desired, they might reason, the private sector will take care of it.

But private markets will not deliver all that is needed in higher education. For example, they will not provide instruction and research in the humanities or the basic sciences, because there is no money to be made in either. These are not trivial intellectual omissions.

Equally important, the methods of evaluating the benefits of education—what economists call "rate of return analysis"—have systematically undervalued the contribution of higher education compared to primary and secondary education. Members of our task force believe this may explain, at least in part, why donors and governments have neglected higher education in the past. We hope that our findings will lead them to reconsider their policies.

The source of the bias stems from the fact that higher education creates valuable public goods that do not enter into the rate-of-return calculations. Higher education, for example, contributes to the spirit of enterprise in a country, to leadership, governance, culture, university research, and democracy. This list can be very long.

I am not suggesting that higher education determines everything within these categories, but if we measure it simply in terms of the additional tax revenues generated by people with education, the other benefits are omitted. The solution is not less primary and secondary education; rather, it is to provide adequate tertiary education.

All types of institutions—public, private, for-profit, and philanthropic—can serve the public interest. But they can do so only if they are part of a national system that sets boundaries, assigns tasks, and assures quality.

Related to the public interest in higher education are forces for social equity. Access for women and for disadvantaged economic and ethnic groups will not be delivered through the profit motive. Access requires some form of public or philanthropic support. Developing countries need to look carefully at the public interest. All types of institutions—public, private, for-profit, and philanthropic—can serve that interest. But they can do so only if they are part of a national system that sets boundaries, assigns tasks, and assures quality. Those responsible for policy cannot simply sit back and let market forces rule.

All too often in developing countries, leaders are ambitious to create an Oxford University or a Free University of Berlin rather than a system to address national problems in higher education. Policymakers should be urged to look at the state of California, which has probably the best comprehensive public system of higher education in this country.

The desirable features of a system are clear. A system must be stratified and tiered, so as to provide both excellence and mass education—all the way from research universities through vocational and distance learning. Ideally, a national system would include public and private institutions—a requirement that creates sensitive political issues. Competition should be encouraged within the categories. There should be well-defined standards for each type of institution, and—this is perhaps a novel suggestion—there should be systemwide resources.

For example, developing countries should set up "learning commons"—such as computer centers, instructional laboratories, and libraries. These facilities would be available to students and faculty at all types of institutions—public, private, for-profit, and not-for-profit—and would enable developing nations to use their higher education investments efficiently. The learning commons should be supervised by the state but not controlled, micromanaged, or politically manipulated.

Having said this, it is easier to understand why, especially among our colleagues in the developing world, governance is such a crucial problem. Especially in countries created after World War II, there often has been little understanding or sympathy for the special needs of higher education—needs not intuitively grasped. It is easier to deal with taxes, the customs system, and road building.

The leaders of developing countries formed after World War II often have had little experience with the needs of higher education. In higher education, the bottom line is difficult to define, individual initiative and creativity must be encouraged, and time horizons for return on investment are much longer than in most other government activities. Moreover, universities—both faculty and students—often present potential political dangers.

> Developing countries should set up "learning commons"—such as computer centers, instructional laboratories, and libraries. These facilities would be available to students and faculty at all types of institutions and would enable developing nations to use their higher education investments efficiently.

To this day in parts of Africa governments appoint and dismiss vice-chancellors, deans, and even department heads absolutely at will. In some countries, the ruling political party appoints vice-chancellors and presidents of universities. In many parts of the former Soviet Union, teachers are voiceless.

The remedies are obvious, but the fact that they are obvious doesn't mean they are easy to implement. There's the tried-and-true: protection of academic freedom; shared governance; selection based on merit; mutually–agreed rights and responsibilities between faculty and the institution, perhaps with an explicit social contract (how I wish we had that in this country!); financial stability; and clear boundaries for students. One is almost embarrassed to read the list because it is so difficult to attain. The problems should not be minimized, but a great deal of work can be done to improve the present situation.

My last two topics relate to curricular issues. The most obvious need is to improve research and teaching in science and technology. The gap in knowledge between rich and poor countries is growing. Western Europe, North America, Japan, and the newly industrialized East Asian countries account for 84 percent of the world's published scientific papers and 97 percent of patents.

We propose that each country should develop its own vision of an educated person, taking into account its own history and culture, and develop a general education curriculum on that basis.

A better scientific base in developing countries is needed not only so these countries can make contributions of their own, but so they can select and adapt existing technologies to local circumstances. For this, higher education is pivotal.

To improve the scientific base in developing nations, it would be helpful to create a global clearinghouse for second-hand equipment, to eliminate import tariffs on scientific equipment, and to apply less stringent intellectual property rules in the developing world. The growing gap between the rich and the poor may in the long run be even more dangerous than HIV.

Our most controversial—even eccentric—topic was a plea for general or liberal education for some students in the developing world. It is eccentric because liberal education is not part of the continental tradition on which most of the universities in the developing are based. In the continental system, general education is assigned to secondary schools, and university training is highly specialized. But we know for a fact that the secondary schools in these countries are no longer capable of providing general education, if they ever were. A second problem is that general education is somewhat elitist and—perhaps at the moment—too American. It requires interactivity and tends to be expensive.

Some people allege that a general education is unresponsive to the needs of the labor market. That is not true. Our proposal is to select the most able students and give them a curriculum aimed at imparting general knowledge and developing general intellectual capacities, focusing on the whole development of those individuals apart from occupational training. We propose that each country should develop its own vision of an educated person, taking into account its own history and culture, and develop a general education curriculum on that basis.

The National University of Singapore recently created a "university scholars" program for the purpose of imparting liberal education. Singapore is not a developing country—it is wealthy—but the exercise of developing the scholars program is a good example for many countries.

The value of general education in poorer countries is obvious. It yields flexibly trained individuals, offers the best training for knowledge-based careers, promotes citizenship and leadership, and provides good preparation for lifelong learning—exactly what is needed.

That value is beginning to be recognized widely. It is interesting, for example, that in Bangladesh, one of the poorest countries in the world, the Bangladesh Rural Advancement Committee is attempting to start a liberal education program. David Frazier, former president of Swarthmore, studied the program:

> While liberal arts education might not be appropriate for the majority of a university-age cohort, or even the majority of those who attend colleges and universities in Bangladesh, it offers some special attributes that could help prepare talented students to be responsible and effective leaders and innovators. These attributes of intellectual independence and initiative, of critical thinking, of creativity, of social responsibility, and of the ability to communicate their ideas to others would be a major benefit to their country.

I will conclude by asking a question. Do we—and here I mean academics from the richer countries, and perhaps especially the leaders of the AAU universities—have any special responsibilities to higher education in the poor countries?

> The value of general education in poorer countries is obvious. It yields flexibly trained individuals, offers the best training for knowledge-based careers, promotes citizenship and leadership, and provides good preparation for lifelong learning— exactly what is needed.

There is an entirely selfish element to an affirmative answer. In a globalized world, the impact of crises becomes greatly magnified. Failure and trouble in the developing world affect us all. Since higher education is so crucial for development, our voices should be loud when it comes to promoting higher education in the developing world.

We have a particular responsibility to place the case for higher education in the developing world before donors, public and private. We should not advocate just for ourselves and ignore 85 percent of the world's population.

The role of higher education in social and economic development is not well understood. AAU members and representatives of similar institutions should lend their support to creating and maintaining real universities—as opposed to what are primarily trade schools and vocational schools—in the developing world. Humanities, basic science, and liberal education are not playthings for the wealthy; they are necessary components of higher education if it is to fulfill its role in development.

H.G. Wells said, "Human history becomes more and more a race between education and catastrophe." Eighty-five percent of the world's population are losing that race.

H.G. Wells said, "Human history becomes more and more a race between education and catastrophe." Eighty-five percent of the world's population are losing that race.

Zhihong Xu is president of Peking University, a position he has held since December 1999, a year after the university celebrated its 100th anniversary.

Located near the Yuan Ming Yuan Garden in Beijing, the university has graduated nearly 100,000 students over those 100 years. Today it is a comprehensive institution offering teaching and research in pure and applied sciences, medical sciences, social sciences and the humanities, and the sciences of management and education.

A plant cell biologist and biotechnologist, Dr. Xu has served as vice-president of the Chinese National Academy of Sciences since October 1992 and chairman of the Chinese Society of Cell Biology since October 1999.

—Charles M. Vest
President, Massachusetts
Institute of Technology

THE ROLE OF UNIVERSITIES IN CHINA'S ECONOMIC DEVELOPMENT

Zhihong Xu
PRESIDENT, PEKING UNIVERSITY

Good afternoon. It is a great pleasure for me to attend the spring meeting of the Association of American Universities. On behalf of Peking University, I congratulate AAU on its 100th anniversary.

Over the past decade, international trade and foreign direct investment have grown much faster than the gross domestic product (GDP) of the nations of the world. With economic barriers dropping as a result of flows in technologies, resources, goods, and services, the world economy is becoming increasingly integrated.

As the most populous country in the world and one of its major economies, China is becoming a significant participant in globalization. In the past two decades, China has pursued a policy of economic openness and reform. Over that twenty-year period, the annual rate of GDP growth has been between 8 and 10 percent, while the annual rate of growth in foreign trade has exceeded 15 percent.

Foreign direct investment also has grown significantly. In 2000, the total volume of China's imports and exports exceeded $474 billion. With China's efforts to enter the World Trade Organization (WTO), the process of economic opening has gained new momentum.

China is committed to globalization because we believe that no one country is able to develop its economy without international cooperation. President Jiang Zeming believes that in China, as in other countries, any attempt to develop a national economy will fail without opening to the rest of the world. China has the will and capacity to be an active and effective player in the world economy.

There are tremendous opportunities for the Chinese economy in integrating into the world economy. China can exploit her comparative advantages, use resources more efficiently, attract more foreign investment, and absorb advanced technologies. Chinese consumers will benefit from lower prices and more variety in foreign goods and services. And China's institutional reforms will accelerate as a result of the transparency and efficiency required by international competition.

But, globalization offers no "free lunch." Every process has its cost. Globalization will raise new issues in economic and social development. Economic efficiency may bring greater social disparities. Because globalization restructures the economy, it creates winners and losers, even if the game is not zero-sum. Some sectors and some countries may be marginalized during this process. Efficiency versus fairness will become a major issue.

Cultural conflict will emerge during economic convergence. When multinational corporations expand their business into different countries, for example, they often bring their own business ethics and social values. These may conflict with the cultural values of local communities.

Economic and cultural development require both competition and cooperation—the key is to develop virtuous rather than vicious competition. The major challenges facing all governments during globalization are how to maximize economic and social benefits, protect cultural diversity, and minimize adjustment costs and social conflicts.

As the largest developing and transitional economy in the world, China has problems unique to its own society. Our population is approaching 1.3 billion, so the ability to meet the ever-increasing demands that come with such numbers is an enormous challenge.

Education in China has a vital role to play in meeting the challenges of globalization. As the most effective weapon in reducing social and economic

> Any attempt to develop a national economy will fail without opening to the rest of the world. But, globalization offers no "free lunch." Every process has its cost.

disparities, education is key to sustaining economic development and long-term prosperity. Accordingly, the Chinese government has developed strategies for revitalizing the nation through science and education.

The major challenges facing all governments during globalization are how to maximize economic and social benefits, protect cultural diversity, and minimize adjustment costs and social conflicts.

Twenty years of hard work have resulted in the dramatic development of Chinese higher education. Last year, 11 million Chinese students were enrolled in higher education. The gross enrollment rate increased from 2 percent in the early 1980s to approximately 11.5 percent today. Enrollment of graduate students increased from 22,000 to 290,000.

To meet China's economic development needs, higher education enrollments will increase to 16 million over the next five years. Even then, because of its large population, China's gross enrollment rate will still be a mere 15 percent. The enrollment of graduate students also will increase, reaching about 600,000 by the end of 2005.

We need to train a new generation of students and leaders to meet the challenges of globalization of the twenty-first century. To communicate with others in the world our students will need not only knowledge and skills in specific areas, but also the ability to adapt to the jobs that come with an advanced economy. At the same time, the fast pace of developments in science and technology means that existing workers will need to continually renew the knowledge they have mastered. Thus, English and computer languages have become the hot fields in Chinese education.

In recent years, many private institutions of higher education have been created in China. The government has encouraged these new institutions to work with foreign universities and businesses to create training courses, such as those leading to a master's in business administration.

After merging last April with Beijing Medical University, one of the largest medical universities in China, Peking University now has about 36,000 students. More than 20 percent of our graduates go abroad each year for further study—most to the United States. About 20,000 Peking University alumni are working or studying in the United States.

To increase the competitiveness of our students in adapting to rapid developments in science and technology, every room in Peking University's student dormitories now has access to the Internet, and classes are increasingly offered through telecommunication networks.

The university also is increasing the diversity of its courses in the humanities, social sciences, technology and engineering, and medical sciences. One example is the double-major program for undergraduate students. Students in the sciences and humanities are taking courses in law and economics that include Western economic theories, comparative institutional studies, and world economic histories, markets, and government. These classes are extremely popular among students and in great demand from companies engaged in foreign trade and joint ventures in China.

But the problems that Henry Rosovsky mentioned in his talk are still present in China. Solving them will require three steps. First, we must attract young talent back to China after they spend a few years in foreign countries. Second, we need to adjust the structure of the university away from the specialized institutes we established in the early 1950s using the model of the former Soviet Union. Third, we need to increase financial support for the universities. In the past five years, the Chinese government has significantly increased the budget for Chinese universities, especially for the top institutions. But it has not spent much money over the past several decades on science education. And despite the overall increases, funding is still short because China is a large country with many universities.

The main goal of education reform in China is to increase the competitiveness of our students in adapting to rapid developments in science and technology.

To meet these challenges, Peking University, over the past twenty years, has established exchange programs with more than 180 universities in forty-nine countries. We have close relationships and collaborations with many universities, including thirty-seven American universities.

At present, the number of overseas students enrolled at the university is about 2,600. Half are undergraduates. The university ranks number one among Chinese universities in this respect. We also have established joint research collaborations with forty universities, including Yale, and companies like IBM and Motorola.

Peking University also is playing a leading role in shaping a new generation of Chinese leaders. Under the pressure of globalization, the Chinese government is undergoing rapid change, reform, and restructuring, with the number of government employees reduced by one-third in the past four years. Higher education and the graduate schools, too, have become a target for institutional reform.

Peking University is well known in China for its cultural diversity and freedom of thought. The schools of economics, management, administration, and even arts have intensive programs for the reeducation of government employees. Currently, we have 8,000 part-time students taking on-the-job training at Peking University. Among them, one-fourth are officials with mid-level or high rank in ministries of regional and local governments. Their renewed knowledge, revived competitiveness, and open-minded attitude will have a tremendous impact on accelerating China's economic advancement.

> Education in China will accelerate the process of creating an open China with economic prosperity, cultural diversity, and social democracy.

We are confident that higher education in China will accelerate the process of creating an open China with economic prosperity, cultural diversity, and social democracy.

To conclude, I would like to tell you a personal story. As a plant biologist, I worked at the Chinese Academy of Sciences for several years after graduating from Peking University in 1965. One-and-a-half years ago I returned as the president of Peking University, the most prestigious university in China and a historical landmark in China's modernization and reform. Our beautiful campus was once the campus of Yenching University and part of Yuan Ming Yuan Garden, the Versailles of China, which was burned down by British and French troops in 1861.

Peking University is a combination of three leading universities in Beijing: Peking University, established in 1898 by the Qing Dynasty emperor; Yenching University, built by American Christians in 1921; and the College of Science and the Liberal Arts of Tsinghua University, created in 1911 by an American program to return China's war reparation payment from the Boxer Rebellion.

Peking University therefore is a product of globalization, revolution, and cultural interactions. Leading it is a major challenge.

Although we paid a high price in the past, we are witnessing progress toward a better, more open world. I hope and trust that the contacts and collaborations between Peking University and universities in the United States and other parts of the world will be strengthened through globalization.

Luis Alfredo Riveros is rector of the University of Chile in Santiago, Chile's oldest and largest university. Educated at the university and at the University of California, Berkeley, he served as professor of economics, chairman of the economics department, and dean of the School of Economics before being elected rector in 1998. His specialties are labor economics and economic development. He has a particular interest and expertise in higher education as it contributes to economic development.

—*Charles M. Vest*
President, Massachusetts
Institute of Technology

THE IMPORTANCE OF UNIVERSITIES TO ECONOMIC DEVELOPMENT AND CULTURAL PRESERVATION IN LATIN AMERICA

Luis Alfredo Riveros
RECTOR, UNIVERSITY OF CHILE

O n behalf of the University of Chile, I would like to express deep gratitude to the Association of American Universities for inviting me to participate in this meeting.

I believe that I speak not only for my own country of Chile, but also for Latin America as an economic, historical, and social entity that is working to fulfill the dream of a better quality of life for its citizens by meeting the challenges of globalization.

The twenty-first century will be an era of internationalization and globalization—and those processes will strongly challenge the university.

First, there is the challenge of preserving local and national cultural identity, even as globalization creates a multicultural world. Through research and the creation of knowledge, universities are expected to be protectors and cultivators of national culture, values, and traditions. That mission will need to take into account the new global scenario.

> Universities are expected to be protectors and cultivators of national culture, values, and traditions.

A second challenge for the university stems from the increasing need to answer multiple, complicated questions in scientific and technological research. In order to tackle these multidisciplinary and often international challenges, academic programs must be better integrated.

A third challenge derives from the fact that the marketplace—with its "competition," "consumer preferences," and "market prices"—is becoming a key element in shaping university development around the world. To some degree, the marketplace is substituting for the role traditionally filled by the state in financing and promoting university activities.

Those challenges will require universities to reexamine their institutional missions, as well as achieve better internal organization and management.

Not only should universities provide the technological knowledge needed for successful and productive globalization, they also should be key actors in tackling the major policy dilemmas involved in that transition. Their research and teaching must help minimize the negative or undesirable effects that may be associated with globalization. That being so, the subject of this opening session will no doubt become a common theme for many university meetings around the world.

Years ago, the concept of economic development was viewed exclusively in terms of growth. We associated different degrees of economic development directly with certain levels of national per capita income.

Today, we accept that economic development involves much more than reaching certain levels of per capita income. Although per capita income is still a key measurement—the current floor of the developed world is around $15,000 to $17,000 American dollars per person per year—other concepts now are indispensable to the definition of economic development, making the concept richer and multidimensional, as it must be to reflect human reality.

Income distribution adds a value judgment to development and should be considered when assessing social welfare. Social welfare, in turn, is intimately linked to the aims of economic development. Following this idea, a "developed" country cannot be one that has a high average income level in combination with great disparities in income distribution.

Another concept in economic development is cultural vitality, which includes ample access to culture. Participation in culture, in this view, must be considered as part of economic and social progress. In the spiritual arena, material progress manifests itself in the valuing of ideas and the appreciation of creativity.

Finally, another indispensable concept in the attainment of economic development is humanism, the profound respect for the person. When respect for the individual is considered an end in itself, and not just a means to attain material wealth, it allows for a society in which diversity, debate, and tolerance—all instruments for sustainable and comprehensive progress—thrive.

Latin America is part of the developing world. Our annual per capita income is between $900 and $7,000. Our region is recognized generally for unequal income distribution, poor access to culture and education, and low valuation of the individual and human life.

While we are part of the world that lags behind, our goal is to become part of the industrialized world in the new century. The task is overwhelming.

We have made sacrifices in recent years to attain sustainable economic programs. We have reformed our economies and liberalized markets across the board. We have radically changed the role and size of the state in the economy and its intervention in social policies. We also have profoundly changed our traditional inward-looking development strategy and opened our trade and capital accounts to the rest of the world.

These reforms have come at substantial cost—high unemployment, dropping real wages, greater disparities in income distribution, inadequate systems of public health and education, deteriorating quality of higher education, and the breakdown of entire industries and productive sectors.

In the end, we have charted a new way toward development—one that is highly dependent on the rest of the world. For example, we have started regional and interregional trade agreements in order to secure markets, promote our own export businesses, and offer new opportunities for investment. But we have suffered great disenchantment because a recession or economic slowdown in any region of the world has more-than-proportionate repercussions on our weak economy. We are still learning about the new meaning of integration and globalization.

There is an increasing tendency in Latin America to view too narrowly the new economic rules, based on what many define as the "new economic order." We still have much to learn about how to run our economies, particularly in completing reforms that will make us eligible for more and better investments. And Latin American nations still have some costs to pay for all the past years of inefficiency and economic distortions.

The answers do not lie in isolated national economic policies or in the traditional system of international relations. In fact, in this new era, both systems merit substantial changes. Human rights protection is one of the most recent examples in which there is widespread support for developing effective international institutions.

One of the issues we face is preparing our national institutions for a more collaborative world. We must evaluate national policies for their likely effects across borders and on international relations.

Additionally, globalization means that some cultural practices and traditions will be stronger or weaker, based on the amount of financial support we can provide for their preservation. Local cultures and simple values should be protected, as should all cultural manifestations, as an endowment of humanity as a whole. Collaboration is vital for protecting valuable cultural inheritances everywhere on the planet.

As economic indicators have improved in Latin America, higher education has generally suffered a drop in quality, one that cannot be reversed with simplistic market policies.

Thus, globalization raises many challenges in the context of three major concerns:

- The need to develop new rules and create new international institutions
- The need to redefine the role and scope of nation-states, particularly by creating a system for better coordination of national policies, and
- The need to protect all cultural traditions, regardless of their levels of local financial support.

All these challenges mean new tasks for the university, which will become more integrated across national borders.

The self-deception in many developing countries about the new economic order largely relates to our failure to understand the need to better balance social and economic policies.

As economic indicators have improved in Latin America, some social indicators have dropped—or have not kept pace. Higher education has generally suffered a drop in quality, one that cannot be reversed with simplistic market policies.

The drop in social indicators may be just a matter of the state setting priorities, or a problem of cutting government spending by too much. Whatever the case—and this is still the subject of economic and political debate—there prevails in our countries the sense that economic progress is limited to the few, that macro-indicators do not reflect the reality of the middle class and the poor, and that perhaps something is wrong with the entire internationalization and globalization process.

It is cruelly ironic that one of the most active counterforces to the globalization process arises from the protectionist policies of the industrialized nations.

That sense of disenfranchisement lies behind the growing protests against globalization and economic integration in developing nations.

It is true that distortions and disruption still prevail in our political and economic relationship with industrialized countries. Industrialized countries buy and invest in our natural resources. But we also would like them to invest in our new industries, which will provide us with sustainable development.

Although the developing world has significantly reduced trade tariffs, the contrary has happened in industrial countries, which have worked together to increase protectionism, a clear failure in making progress in multilateral trade.

Not only is protectionism unfair, but it is inconsistent with globalization, which is supposed to offer a better world for all. It is cruelly ironic that one of the most active counterforces to the globalization process arises from the protectionist policies of the industrialized nations.

Thus, successful globalization will demand both the redesign of international policies and improvements in the system of international relations. Such a redesign must attend to social demands and develop human resources and social infrastructure around the world. It also must lead to new agreements and international regulations that foster healthy economic integration. To ensure efficiency, economic integration should include the deregulation of all three markets: products, capital, and labor.

What are the risks if such changes are not made? First, there is the risk of returning to a world of trade protectionism and distortions. This would run counter to current developments in technology and communications and worsen market inefficiencies by deepening the technological divide and stunting markets needed to sustain economic growth.

Second, there is the risk of creating a larger social and economic divide. A continuing world of big winners and big losers will create tremendous political conflicts.

Third, there is the risk of introducing an unbalanced world culture characterized by the destruction of local and national cultural traditions. Although the world's people would seem closer to one another, those in many geographical regions would feel ignored and frustrated.

A continuing world of big winners and big losers will create tremendous political conflicts.

As we look at significant changes in technology and communications, we often believe that their results are unavoidable. That may be true, but we must use our collective wisdom to create the conditions for a more humane world.

The university has a significant role to play in such efforts. As part of its long evolution from medieval Europe, the university serves as the think tank of a nation: providing independent thought, encompassing a variety of interests, and promoting academic excellence.

By definition the university is multidisciplinary. It can look at issues in a comprehensive way. It can use the best researchers and educators to find ways to ease the problems associated with globalization.

And the university is the repository and protector of a nation's culture. As such, it requires adequate government resources to protect and enhance culture even as it helps society prepare for globalization. The government must finance these university tasks because the marketplace will not support them.

In many ways, developing countries have been losing the tradition of this sort of university, the very kind that is needed in the era of globalization.

In conclusion, if we want to live in a better world—a world that is largely dependent upon technological and scientific progress—we need to restore our universities as the true brain of our societies and the soul of the future of humanity. Thank you very much.

SESSION DISCUSSION

MR. VEST: I now open the floor to anyone who would like to comment or ask a question.

SABIH TANSAL, Rector, Bogazici University, Istanbul: I would like to comment on Professor Rosovsky's statement about the Turkish university. He gave a very poor example.

The typical Turkish university has between 10,000 and 20,000 students. Anadolu University is a distance-learning institution that attracts only students who cannot score high enough on the central exam to attend another university.

MR. ROSOVSKY: I did characterize Anadolu as a distance-learning institution. I am aware that it is an open university.

MR. TANSAL: It is not a typical Turkish university.

MR. ROSOVSKY: I was not implying that it was.

PETER GAEHTGENS, President, Free University of Berlin: I also would like to ask a question about Professor Rosovsky's lecture, which I found intriguing and moving. In fact, I think you are challenging the group assembled here.

The question is, "What is the conclusion?" You said that the North-South gap was increasing and that the gap between the educational systems in developed and developing countries was increasing. What conclusions should we, who represent institutions that call themselves research universities and form particular clubs within the general systems of higher education, draw from those assertions?

You did not mention the issue of research. We believe that research is an essential part of higher education. In most of the countries about which you reported, research generally is in a worse situation than education.

I wonder whether the group of universities assembled here should take action in this respect? If it is true that the private sector will not support the work in developing countries that is required to make the gap smaller, maybe institutions like ours should take the initiative.

I would like to challenge you to consider consequences rather than only reporting the unfortunate facts.

MR. ROSOVSKY: Thank you, sir. That's a very unfair question, you have to admit. I like to think of myself as a diagnostician. I don't have many cures at my disposal.

Let me deal with two issues that you raise. We all realize that the situation varies enormously from country to country. Technically China is a developing country. But you can't compare China—with its history, culture, and economic growth—with many of the other developing countries.

We do believe that research is crucial, but not in every institution, and that is why I spoke about systems. The system issue is very important and underappreciated in many parts of the world. But somewhere there has to be a research effort, and since you are from the University of Berlin, I can say that that effort must exist for "Humboldtian" reasons. The value placed on independent scholarship and research is universal at the top tier of institutions.

But what is to be done to improve recognition of higher education with research at its apex?

If we agree with the diagnosis that higher education is crucial in the developing world, the group here today could influence donor agencies and international organizations. For example, it would be a good idea for universities in a variety of countries to develop a form of Peace Corps to work in certain parts of the world. Maybe AAU or an international organization could initiate such an effort.

Competition is fine, but it is not the best way to create new universities.

A great deal of good can be done simply by talking to our colleagues in different parts of the world. In Africa and parts of the former Soviet Union, our colleagues feel extremely isolated, as if nobody cares about them. But there are people taking action. I notice that His Highness the Aga Khan is in the audience. He has done exemplary things in higher education in parts of the world where I'm sure many people felt as if nobody cared until he and his organization showed up.

MR. VEST: I wonder if President Xu or Rector Riveros would like to comment on this issue of research at universities in your nations.

MR. RIVEROS: I think research is fundamental for any university. Professor Rosovsky told us about the "garage universities" in El Salvador. In many developing countries, particularly in Latin America, it has been popular to increase the number of these "universities" as part of a political attempt—often with the recommendation of international organizations—to create competition. Competition is fine, but it is not the best way to create new universities.

In Chile, for instance, the number of universities has increased from eight to sixty-four. We don't have the human resources to support them seriously.

In financing these schools, research has suffered. There is little money for scientific research, and there is no money for research in social science and humanities.

If we want to expand universities—which is fine, because it is a good idea to have more people studying at universities—we need first to invest in developing the human resources to support them. It also would be good to differentiate between universities and other institutions of higher education such as colleges, which in our countries are very difficult to differentiate.

MR. XU: In China, scientific research is still a problem, even for the top universities. Foreign visitors sometimes mention that the university is quite good at certain types of research. But compared with the top universities in the Western world, there is still a great gap.

In recent years, many young people have come back to China from the United States, the European countries, and Japan. Not only are they improving the quality of research, but also they are helping us restructure the university and its departments. That's very important.

Because I have worked in the sciences for years, my experience is that when you initiate a special project, especially in basic research, the best way is to set up a collaboration between researchers in your country and those from developed countries. We have experience in working on projects in China with scientists from the United States, Japan, and other countries. In those projects that really boost science and technology development, scientists get together, study the problem, and use the results for social and economic development.

Most importantly for such collaborations in developing countries, local scientists must be included. Not only do local scientists better understand local needs and conditions, but their participation in the research helps improve their own research activities. In visiting several developing countries, I have found that when scientists from the developed world fail to include local scientists in their work, their projects generally are less successful for local economic development.

When scientists from the developed world fail to include local scientists in their work, their projects generally are less successful for local economic development.

MR. ROSOVSKY: The key issue is reversing the brain drain. The country that has done best in that regard is probably India. When you look at India you immediately focus on the Indian Institutes of Technology. Created with the participation of foreign partners, the institutes have done a remarkable job in bringing educated people back to India.

MATTHEW LUHANGA, Vice-Chancellor, University of Dar Es Salaam, Tanzania: Many changes have begun in African universities, so the story isn't quite as bleak as it has been presented here.

Just last April, four foundations in the United States—Ford, Rockefeller, MacArthur, and Carnegie—launched a joint effort to support African universities that are making reforms. They started with three universities, but their intention is to keep increasing the number. The initial funding was $100 million, but as the number of universities increases they are approaching partners in Europe for additional support.

There also are efforts in Europe, some of which have been going on for more than two decades, that support research and research training in African universities.

My colleague from Germany will be pleased to note that the engineering program at the University of Dar es Salaam was created by the German government. It has been one of the German government's largest projects in Tanzania. Although that assistance has ended, the reforms that were started in the engineering project have continued.

So positive things are taking place in Africa. But linkages are very important. If we focus on older professors who have done no research for fifteen years because of the lack of funds, we might be wasting our time.

Instead, we should invest in young people by sending them abroad to work with good scientists. When they return with their doctoral degrees, we should support those young scientists, and we will be creating a foundation for longer-term, sustainable research in our institutions.

Before I make a few more points about what Professor Rosovsky said, I would like to thank the Association of American Universities for inviting me to this conference. I must admit that when I saw the letter of invitation I was a bit surprised because we have an Association of African Universities. When I saw the "AAU," I thought I was invited to attend that association. But I was glad that I was invited to this one, and that I was able to come.

Professor Rosovsky, you made two important points. I would like to add one—an item that didn't come up very clearly in your presentation—on the increasing number of students from secondary school who are seeking higher education opportunities but for whom places are not available. A new issue in Africa is the increasing number of offshore providers of higher education. The largest number of MBA holders in Africa have degrees from the Open University of the United Kingdom rather than from any single African university. We are seeing a flood of offshore providers of higher education. That is a fairly new phenomenon.

Regarding liberal education, we found that, due to the legacy we inherited from the colonial era and the linkages we had with our colleagues in the United Kingdom, the syllabi we had were very prescriptive. They defined in detail, almost up to the last course, what a student had to take. So we're trying to make our degree programs a bit more flexible by asking, "What is the core?" We want to give even engineering students, medical students, and others greater flexibility—and access to liberal arts courses.

A new issue in Africa is the increasing number of offshore providers of higher education.

Just as 85 percent of the world's population lives in developing countries, within developing countries about 85 percent of the people live in rural areas. Thus, the immediate impact of change for rural dwellers may come from regionalization rather than from global trends.

I would like to emphasize another point that Professor Rosovsky made. We can learn from one another, even if we are in developing countries. For example, in deregulation of the telecommunications and power sectors, we learned more from the rural telecommunications models in Chile than we did from the American or British models. In the power sector, we learned a great deal from the experience in Bolivia. Maybe that was because the rural telephone sectors in the United States and Britain are not as significant as those in Chile.

PETER MCPHERSON, President, Michigan State University: Professor Rosovsky, you mentioned early in your comments that a major problem for universities around the world is governance. That is why, some twenty-five years ago, the World Bank and the U.S. Agency for International Development (USAID) cut back their work with universities, except for specialized programs in areas such as agriculture and engineering.

I support the World Bank getting back into this area, but I do think that governance issues are the most challenging. What do you think should be the role of donor agencies and foundations in governance, since that historically has been a local issue?

MR. ROSOVSKY: I know that the word "conditionality" is not welcomed anywhere. I certainly do not believe, for example, that U.S. practices of governance should be imposed on the rest of the world. Nothing has a stronger cultural component than governance. But there is a need for much more education about governance. These are issues that people haven't thought about much. Why is it that political groups take such an active role inside universities? Has the case ever been made that academic freedom has a considerable payoff?

I was not aware of the point that you made about the World Bank and USAID pulling back from support of universities. I'm sure it's correct. I did not realize that governance was the reason why international groups backed away.

I am aware, of course, of the Carnegie Institution's effort in Africa. I don't know whether they have concerns about governance, but it is a very important point.

JURGEN MLYNEK, President, Humboldt University of Berlin: Among the five topics that you mentioned, Professor Rosovsky, there was science and technology and then, as the last one, general and liberal education. My question deals with how much attention we pay to science versus the humanities. If you look at developed countries like the United States and some countries in Europe, the role and the importance of humanities in the universities is losing importance. Science is considered to be more important.

On the other hand, there is the question that was addressed by our colleague from Chile, who said that national identity was important to maintain in the process of globalization. I feel that the role of humanities in the developing countries, especially given the concern to preserve national identity, might be even more important than in the developed countries.

MR. ROSOVSKY: I am not a humanist. Chuck Vest already revealed that I practiced the "dismal science" for many years. But I cannot agree with you more. The humanities in U.S. universities are facing very hard times. Our institutions are more and more subject to the marketplace and to pressure to create profit centers. I am gratified that both Dr. Xu and Dr. Riveros supported general education.

Let me make one more point regarding the continental tradition. The question is not "science" versus "general education." General education has a science component for those who are not going to be scientists. That is an important point. But I agree completely with the thrust of your remark.

JACQUES MARCOVITCH, Rector, University of São Paulo, Brazil: Do you see the new generation of those born around 1980 as a continuation of the previous generation, only slightly changed, or are we confronting a dramatic change in the mentality of young people? If such change is happening, what are the implications for higher education?

MR. ROSOVSKY: I don't know exactly what you are referring to. Do you mean that the post–1980 generation grew up on the Internet and, therefore, is more used to working alone?

We have been in existence since medieval times and we have changed all the time. That we should suddenly lose our capacity for change is a great misconception.

I am very conservative. I believe that the visions people are drawing for us are highly simplistic and very implausible. I once gave a talk at Rice University in which I described what Harvard would look like in twenty-five years. I said that Widener Library would be an old-age home because we wouldn't need books and students. The president's mansion would be the biggest McDonald's in the world. Courses were going to be imported from everywhere. Israel would do computer science and we would do personal injury law, and so forth.

It's amusing. But I don't believe it for a moment. Peter Drucker said not long ago, "The campus is finished. Nobody needs it." As somebody mentioned, we have been in existence since medieval times—and I'm quite sure there was a university in China before medieval times—and we have changed all the time. That we should suddenly lose our capacity for change is a great misconception.

In fact, I don't know of anything that changes as continually as fine universities. The changes will not be revolutionary; they will be evolutionary. Education will always have a strong social component—and staring at a screen is not going to replace the interaction involved in teaching and research.

> Education will always have a strong social component—and staring at a screen is not going to replace the interaction involved in teaching and research.

We must change. I fully understand that. But I want us to change without throwing out the baby with the bath water. That would be a good slogan for the twenty-first century.

MR. VEST: The worst future I can conjure up is that we try to determine who is the best lecturer in the world in each subject and then put their lectures out on the Internet so that every student in the world sits in front of the box and listens to the same set of talking heads. That's exactly where some of the early thinkers about Internet education began. It would be terrible. Fortunately it will not happen.

I believe—and I am very proud that the faculty of my institution have recently come to the same conclusion—that the real, bedrock use of the Internet by research institutions should be to publish materials for teachers everywhere to pick up, fit together, and adopt as they see fit. Then, in turn, we should put up on the Internet the material that those teachers develop. That way, we can have a global sharing that allows teachers to adopt material and use it locally as they see fit.

I also want to comment about the coming generation. Sociological studies here in the United States show, perhaps to our surprise, that young people now entering universities or about to enter universities have a much greater sense than their predecessors of working together cooperatively and forming teams. It's quite different from the trends of the past few years.

Three years ago, my colleagues at the Media Laboratory at MIT spent a year hooking up 2,000 to 3,000 young people—early teenagers of twelve, thirteen, and fourteen years of age—on the Internet so that they could talk with each other. The students were enlisted from all over the world, with an emphasis on people living in developing countries and developing regions. We asked each of them to provide a short essay on how new technologies could improve the quality of life in their regions.

Through a voting system, they selected 100 of their own members to spend a week together at MIT. One of the students' activities was to develop a manifesto, which they presented at the end of the week to a group of leaders from industry, academia, and government. The number one item on their manifesto was, "We must preserve our local and national cultures."

That was heartwarming and encouraging, especially coming from people from all over the world who know how to use these technologies.

KAARE NORUM, Rector, University of Oslo, Norway: You mentioned, Dr. Rosovsky, that a key question was how to get students back to China. We from research universities in the developed world have many excellent graduate students and young scientists from the developing world on our campuses. You were saying that India was very clever to get its students back. Is there something that we at research universities can do to send the students and the scientists from developing countries back and then form collaborations with them? There is a tendency for research universities to keep the best students and young scientists. Did your report discuss that?

MR. ROSOVSKY: We discussed this primarily from the point of view of countries creating an atmosphere that makes people want to come back. That has a lot to do with the political situation and the financing of research and higher education. U.S. immigration laws force many graduates to leave, but the main burden will always be on the home country. Most students want to return home if conditions are tolerable.

I agree with the thrust of your question, but I haven't got a policy to suggest.

MR. XU: In China, the government recently has increased the budget for universities and institutes. That is the most important factor in convincing young people to return to China. A second factor is that we are encouraging young people who come back to China to stay current with new ideas and technologies in the West by helping them maintain their contacts and collaborations with the foreign labs where they worked or studied. In fact, several of my former Ph.D. students are now back in China.

We are encouraging young people who come back to China to stay current with new ideas and technologies in the West by helping them maintain their contacts and collaborations with the foreign labs where they worked or studied.

For example, Peking University and China's academic science institutes are collaborating with German universities and the Max Planck Society in Germany on several joint laboratory partnerships in China. One of my former Ph.D. students spent two or three months a year in Germany and the rest of his time back in China. In his case, that made a strong collaborative project work and improved a research laboratory in China. We can learn a lot from such collaborations.

MR. RIVEROS: I agree that financial resources are an important dimension, but there is also the problem of having a critical mass of students for interaction and feedback in the country. In China and India it probably is possible to have a critical mass because of the size of the university population. But in the smaller countries it is very difficult because there are just two or three specialists in a certain area.

International collaboration is the place to use the new communications technologies to create better worldwide interaction for certain disciplines. In this way, we can have people return to their country to work, do research, and teach, and still have access to the latest developments in their disciplines.

ARTHUR KWOK-CHEUNG LI, Vice-Chancellor, the Chinese University of Hong Kong: In regard to the brain-drain issue, all universities would like to have brain gain, as would the education ministries in all developing countries. But the problem really starts in the developing countries. When their young people receive postgraduate education overseas they are exposed to different concepts, governments, and ways of life. If one or two come back, that's fine. But when there is a mass return of these young people with very different ideas, that's when the trouble can start.

3

SHARED ISSUES
IN INTERNATIONAL
HIGHER EDUCATION

APRIL 22, 2001

INTRODUCTION

Charles M. Vest

PRESIDENT, MASSACHUSETTS INSTITUTE OF TECHNOLOGY

I t gives me the greatest pleasure to introduce this evening's speaker. I have had the privilege of knowing His Highness the Aga Khan for many years. One of his many important contributions to education is a program of advanced study in Islamic architecture based at Harvard and MIT.

He is a unique figure on the international scene. His Highness is the forty-ninth hereditary Imam of the Shia Imami Ismaili Muslims, a community that resides in some twenty-five countries—mainly in west, central, and south Asia, eastern Africa, the Middle East, North America, and Western Europe.

He emphasizes that Islam is a thinking, spiritual faith—one that teaches compassion and tolerance and upholds the dignity of human beings.

Through the private philanthropy of the agencies collectively known as the Aga Khan Development Network, he has enabled the very poor in Asia and Africa to enhance their lives through programs that focus on primary health care, education, housing, and social and economic development.

The Aga Khan's many contributions to education in the developing world include the establishment of the Aga Khan University, the first private university in Pakistan.

To date, the university has concentrated on research and professional education in the fields of health care and education. It recently announced plans to add an undergraduate college of arts and sciences to its offerings in Karachi. The university also is establishing an advanced nursing program in East Africa.

Continuing his efforts on behalf of higher education, last year His Highness signed an international treaty with the presidents of Kazakhstan, Kyrgyzstan, and Tajikistan to create the University of Central Asia. This will be the first university in the world devoted to research and teaching on the issues facing mountain peoples in the settings in which they live.

His role in both these institutions goes beyond that of catalyst and benefactor. His Highness is the chancellor of the Aga Khan University and the chancellor-designate of the University of Central Asia.

The Aga Khan is committed to improving understanding between western and Muslim cultures and between the developed and developing worlds.

The Aga Khan Trust for Culture supports programs designed to enrich the training of professionals in Islamic architecture and related fields. And the Aga Khan University is developing an Institute of Islamic Civilizations in London.

One of the Aga Khan's special interests is the way in which new information technologies can be used in the service of education and development. To that end, he is exploring the use of the Internet to enable institutions to share scarce resources, to bridge cultural and physical distances to create new educational and professional communities, and to give voice to groups and peoples who traditionally have been unheard.

In this, as in all his endeavors, he brings a unique global perspective and profound belief in the importance of education to our collective future.

Making a Difference: Reflections on Shared Problems, Opportunities, and Responsibilities in International Higher Education

His Highness the Aga Khan
Forty-Ninth Hereditary Imam of the Shia Imami Ismaili Muslims

T hank you, President Vest, for your very generous words of introduction, and thank you all for the very warm welcome. It is an
honor to be invited to address such a distinguished group of educators. If IQ could be converted into kilowatts, I have no doubt that the quan-
tum massed here tonight would meet the world's energy requirements for at
least a decade.

In 1954 I came to the United States for the first time and entered
Harvard College as a first-year student. It was an experience that I will never
forget. All of my formal education up to that point had been in French.
Although I had studied English, my command of the language was not up to
the demands of Harvard's curriculum. Fortunately several of us in the same
position worked together to find French editions of as many of the assigned

readings as possible. We wrote our papers in French, translated them into English, and waited in fear for our grades.

By a quirk of nature, although I was born right-handed, I had the good fortune to come into this world left-footed. Soccer players who could kick with their left foot were very rare in the United States in those days. This meant that I was able to make the freshman soccer team as the left wing. We were a distinguished group. We turned in an undefeated season and had the distinction of being placed on a list in the dean's office—not to be confused with the dean's list, although we never troubled to explain that fine distinction fully to our parents. To this day, I am convinced that I owe my Harvard degree to my left foot.

I can tell you that I had many a sleepless night during that first year at Harvard, and when sleep came, it was often accompanied by a dream (nightmare might be more accurate). In it I was hauled up in front of a senior authority figure, thoroughly scolded about my performance, told that I was unfit to be a member of the Harvard community of scholars, and then sent back to my room to pack my bag to return home. Not knowing anything about the structure of educational institutions other than my boarding school in Switzerland, I always imagined that authority figure to be the head of the institution, or in the case of Harvard, its president. Memories of the fear I felt at having to face only one university president, then, gave me little comfort as I prepared to face a room full of you here tonight.

As I turned my thoughts to what I might say on this occasion, that old fear took on a new form. How could I presume to have something to present on the subject of higher education that was worthy of the scholarship, experience, and responsibilities represented in this room? I am not trained as an academic, published as a scholar, or experienced as an educational administrator. So although I am not sure that my comments will fulfil the program committee's expectations, I have decided to draw on my experience working in social and economic development in parts of Asia and Africa over the last forty years.

Several of the issues about which I will speak were touched on by the Task Force on Higher Education convened two years ago by the World Bank and UNESCO, a task force co-chaired by Professor Henry Rosovsky, who spoke to us so effectively this afternoon. I will illustrate and expand on those issues by drawing on the experience of the agencies that comprise the Aga Khan Development Network. They have worked in areas with high concentrations of the world's poor in Central and South Asia, and in Sub-Saharan Africa. The purpose is not to toot our own horn, but to focus on specific problems and opportunities. I also will offer examples and lessons that can be drawn from our experience working in circumstances that are often very difficult due to the collapse of economies, political instability, and civil strife. I hope to convince institutions in both the developing and the industrialized world to come together to work on common problems, opportunities, and responsibilities.

For those not familiar with our work, I would note that while the Aga Khan Development Network's activities are rooted in the worldwide Shia Ismaili Muslim community, its programs and activities in each setting are open to all without regard to ethnicity, race, gender, or religion. As a matter of policy, none of the network's educational institutions offer instruction in religion unless required by the national curriculum.

Quality education at all levels is, and has been, critically important for all societies. In the developing world, education offers the poor opportunities for new futures: for women, higher status and new roles in their families and communities; for migrants, an asset that is portable; and for refugees, an asset that is both portable and secure. For these reasons, the Aga Khan Education Service has for many years operated several hundred schools in East Africa and Central and South Asia—many in isolated settings, and many with a particular interest in the education of girls.

I mention this because the rest of my remarks this evening will focus on higher education, and I do not want to be understood, even by implication, as believing that primary and secondary school are of lesser significance. They are critical to the existence of an informed citizenry everywhere. Quality school-level education is particularly important in the developing world, where only a small percentage of the population will ever be able to attend a university, and where population growth is massively more rapid than the expansion of capacity of its universities. Finally, the school system has a vital role to play in preparing those who do go on for further studies to make full use of that opportunity. It is the supply system for higher education and therefore cannot be neglected.

But higher education has a special importance because of the difference it can make by developing new models and standards for other institutions in society, and by inculcating in its students the skills of critical thinking, analysis, and problem solving, underpinned by a strong grasp of moral reasoning, ethics, and respect for others.

While our world may be changing at a rate unprecedented in human history, the change is not all positive. Change is disrupting many societies, as evidenced by the violence that we see in so many parts of the world today. Positive change that is permanent requires strong institutions at all levels of society, and institutional development requires models and capable, enlightened leadership.

Higher education has a special importance because of the difference it can make by developing new models and standards for other institutions in society.

The report of the Task Force on Higher Education makes some important observations and recommendations in its review of higher education in the developing world. Among the most important from my perspective are those that relate to higher education as a public good and the reevaluation of the public returns on investment in higher education. Those findings support the task force's recommendation for greater investment in higher education in the developing world by governments, international development organizations, and private initiatives.

The questions most commonly asked when people learn that I am founding a new university are: "How many students will it have?" and "When will the construction of buildings begin?" From my perspective the questions should be:

- Given all the current problems in that country, and all the existing universities, why start another university?
- What will it teach?
- What are your expectations for the impact that the institution and its graduates will have?
- How secure is its funding over time?

Institutions of higher education offer greater prospects of success to their students and the societies they serve when they focus on four factors: quality, relevance, impact, and resources.

The decision more than twenty years ago to create the Aga Khan University (or AKU, as we refer to it) as the first private university in Pakistan was taken in the context of the deteriorating quality of higher education in the developing world. As a private university, AKU would have to remain small, but to justify the investment required it would have to become a role model for a country of more than 120 million people. To assume and retain this status, AKU had to be a quality institution not only in terms of its academic offerings, but also in terms of admission and financial aid policies, governance, management, and financial health. Attracting board members of international standing in fields of education and development played a critical role in this quest.

We achieved academic excellence through careful selection of faculty and by nurturing partnerships with important institutions in the West, many of which are represented in this room—Harvard, Johns Hopkins, McMaster, Toronto, Oxford—and in Asia with the National University of Singapore.

But quality is not enough to justify the support of donors, society, and the authorities in a developing country—a university's offerings must also be relevant. Following a study carried out with the assistance of Harvard, AKU's board decided to focus its initial efforts on addressing the very poor quality of social services in Pakistan and much of the developing world. Today, the Faculty of Health Sciences, including Nursing and the Institute for Educational Development, are all having an impact beyond the training of students at high levels in their respective fields. They have given new status and recognition to women professionals who constitute the overwhelming majority of teachers and nurses in the region.

The Medical College's Health Sciences Department has developed a pioneering model that treats the community as well as the individuals who present themselves for care. A fifth of the medical curriculum is in the community health sciences. Nursing students also study community health and obtain their learning experiences in the rural areas of the country.

The quality and impact of the university is further revealed by the fact that over the last fifteen years, Pakistan's professional licensing body has recommended that all medical colleges in Pakistan adopt AKU's model of community-based medical education. Similarly, the Pakistan Nursing Council has adopted AKU's nursing curriculum.

Research also has concentrated on themes that have outcomes that benefit society. More than half of all course participants in the university's Institute for Educational Development come from government institutions. The institute's impact is visible not only in improvements to classrooms and management of government schools, but also in the government's major policymaking forums, in which the institute is regularly invited to participate.

This is the kind of role that a small, private university with strong international connections can play if it focuses on quality, relevance, and impact—and if it seeks opportunities to share its experience and human resources with other institutions and with society as a whole. Examples, models, and well-trained graduates can help improve the performance of the vast number of schools, universities, health clinics, and hospitals in countries like Pakistan. They are necessary to meet the country's needs but often function at levels far below their potential.

I would now like to shift to another area of great importance for higher education in the developing world—the rapid advances in communications and information technology of the last ten to fifteen years. Those advances have opened up the prospect of dramatically expanding international linkages and the reach of educational programs in both spatial and temporal terms. This topic is on tomorrow's agenda—appropriately so for an international gathering of educational leaders.

The ability to project programs and activities over great distances can bring educational opportunities and resources into settings where they are poorly developed because of financial constraints or sheer isolation.

The effects of communications and information technologies on the role, structure, and functioning of the university as we have known it are only beginning to emerge. But the development of those technologies is important for universities everywhere in the world, even though applications may vary for some time to come.

The ability to project programs and activities over great distances can bring educational opportunities and resources into settings where they are poorly developed because of financial constraints or sheer isolation. Where individuals have access to computers in their homes or—as will be the case in rural areas in developing countries for some time to come—in community centers, technology can provide the first real opportunity for lifelong education on a broad scale.

One lesson is clear. The mastery of the essential elements of information and communications technologies will have to be part of the experience of every university student sooner rather than later. The use of the technology should have a place in the educational process itself, and its mastery should be on the list of competencies that every graduate should possess.

But this is only the first step. Even in the United States—the leader in the development and application of information and communications technologies—the realization of their potential for education is still at a very early stage. A few weeks ago, Lawrence Grossman, former president of NBC News and the Public Broadcasting Service (PBS), and Newton Minow, former chairman of the Federal Communications Commission and PBS, made this point in an op-ed piece entitled "The U.S. Should Invest in a Digital Library" that appeared in the *International Herald Tribune*. They introduce the recommendation in the article's title by observing that "the Internet and digital communication are being largely wasted in America as a resource for the kind of broad education the future demands.... Entertainment of marginal quality dominates commercial attempts on the Internet to reach a mass audience," while at the same time "the treasures in U.S. libraries, schools, and museums are locked away for want of money to make them available to the full American audience."

I have quoted this article at some length not to advocate Grossman's and Minow's solution—although I think it makes great sense for the United States and would also be a priceless gift to the rest of the world and to the cause of world peace—but because it so clearly and authoritatively makes the case for concrete and imaginative steps that may lead to a fuller utilization of the Internet for educational purposes.

What is needed is not a single cosmic solution, but a wide range of initiatives. The Internet was created at an international research institute in Switzerland as a means to make data and findings readily available without cost to scientists around the world. Institutions of higher education have a responsibility to participate in developing and shaping the use of the Internet for educational purposes in their societies and around the world.

At a seminar on architectural education in Switzerland in early April, William Mitchell, dean of the School of Planning and Architecture at the

Massachusetts Institute of Technology and an authority on the various uses of the Internet, offered a succinct summary of some of the advantages and disadvantages of using the Internet for remote education. The debate over conventional versus remote education is wrongly formulated, he suggested. The issues are their relative advantages and disadvantages—including effectiveness and cost—and their complementary use.

Remote education is disadvantaged because it does not offer the value-added that comes from proximity to the instructor and from cross-fertilization with other students in the classroom or studio. Because users need facilities and training to draw on remote education and shape it to their needs, it carries high overheads, particularly at the outset. On the positive side, remote education offers advantages of scale. It dramatically increases the reach to scattered rural communities, which still represent the vast majority of the developing world's population. It adds the possibility of bringing imported expertise into remote and isolated contexts. It creates opportunities for cross-cultural experiences. And it makes possible the broad collaboration of specialists in scattered locations.

Dean Mitchell contends that efforts to combine distance education with classroom learning can reap the benefits of what he calls "educationally mediated globalization," which respects and incorporates intellectual diversity and cultural pluralism.

Examples are more meaningful than generalizations. I will offer two rather different examples of efforts by agencies of the Aga Khan Development Network to make more effective use of the Internet for educational purposes.

The first is a project to develop a World Wide Web–based resource to enrich the architectural information available to students, teachers, scholars, and professionals in the Islamic world. It builds on twenty-five years of cultural research, education, and revitalization by the Aga Khan Programme for Islamic Architecture at Harvard and MIT, and the programs of what is now the Aga Khan Trust for Culture in Geneva.

These initiatives were launched following a series of consultations with architectural scholars and professionals of all faiths and from different parts of the world who came together to address a black hole in Islamic societies with respect to one of the most important dimensions of their identity and heritage: their built environment. At that time there was a real vacuum—very little scholarship, no centers for study or professional training, and there were no collections of visual and textual resources on one of history's greatest traditions of architecture. Improving the quality of life, many seemed to believe, demanded that we adopt the symbolism and style of countries and societies that were considered advanced.

Twenty-five years later a complete turnaround has been achieved. Not only have patrons and professionals come to understand and embrace this important form of cultural expression, but the inventories of buildings in different countries have revealed and legitimated a diversity of expression of which even those living in the Islamic world were unaware.

The emergence of the World Wide Web as a vehicle allows these efforts in public and professional education of the last twenty-five years to take on an entirely new scale. The project, called ArchNet, is being developed at MIT and is scheduled for launch in September 2001. ArchNet will bring together and make available the visual and textual information amassed in collections in Cambridge and Geneva. Though microscopic in comparison, it is an example of just the kind of digitization of inaccessible material for which Grossman and Minow are arguing.·

Improving the quality of life, many seemed to believe, demanded that we adopt the symbolism and style of countries and societies that were considered advanced.

But the example does not stop here. It is not enough to simply dump information into communities around the world, even if, as in this case, they are communities of trained professionals. The ArchNet website provides space for users to exhibit their own work, to communicate with other ArchNet members, to participate in informal discussions of topics of their choice that are relevant to the overall purpose of the project, and to participate in organized discussions, including collaborative design studios. Equally important, schools and departments of architecture with interests in the Islamic world can establish sections on the site to present their programs, activities, and collections of visual and textual materials.

In ArchNet's development phase, institutions from Malaysia, India, Pakistan, Turkey, Lebanon, Egypt, and Jordan were invited to help establish this dimension of the website. Once it is officially open, other institutions may join as well. A special effort will be made to bring in schools of architecture in Central Asia and Sub-Saharan Africa.

My second example relates to the new University of Central Asia. Last summer, on behalf of the Ismaili Imamat, I signed an international treaty founding the university with the presidents of Tajikistan, Kyrgyzstan, and Kazakhstan. The university will make a significant contribution to peace and stability in the largely forgotten mountain zone of Inner Asia by addressing some of the most important problems that plague it—poverty, isolation, and a deep sense of hopelessness.

Dedicated to addressing the problems of poverty, underdevelopment, and environmental degradation, the University of Central Asia will provide training and research on the problems and prospects of the 20 to 30 million people who inhabit the mountainous areas of Central Asia. The new institution, which will begin by offering continuing education courses this year, will be private and secular. It will recruit students and faculty on the basis of merit and will be open equally to men and women. Its main campus will be based in southeastern Tajikistan, in the town of Khorog on the Panj River, which serves as the international boundary between Tajikistan and Afghanistan. Satellite campuses will be opened in mountain settings in Kyrgyzstan and Kazakhstan, and in other countries in the region that decide to join the university in the years ahead.

The University of Central Asia will provide training and research on the problems and prospects of the 20 to 30 million people who inhabit the mountainous areas of Central Asia.

Given the university's sites and mission, it has no option but to make aggressive use of the latest developments in information and communications technologies. This is particularly true for its degree programs, which will start with a master's degree in integrated mountain studies in three years and a bachelor's degree soon thereafter. These programs will be taught in English. They will draw heavily on databases and human resources specialized in mountain studies, to supplement the locally recruited and specially trained instructional staff.

A small, dedicated, but widely scattered group of specialists around the world is committed to the study of mountains and mountain populations. Self-identified as the "mountain mafia," their experience and knowledge will provide the kind of remote resource that can be imported, and their interaction with students and faculty, during summer visits and throughout the year on a rotating basis, will lay the foundation for the kind of "mediated cross-cultural dialogue" that Dean Mitchell envisions.

There is one last topic about which I would like to say a few words. Building capacity for moral reasoning and moral judgment is a goal that appears in the foundation documents of many of the world's oldest and most prestigious universities. For several reasons, I worry that insufficient attention is being paid to the development of these important capabilities. And I worry that the situation may worsen in the years ahead.

> The complexities of world problems and societies today require people educated in broad humanistic traditions in addition to the guidance and direction provided by the teaching of their religion.

The advances that have occurred in the sciences—most recently in the biological sciences and in the engineering that underlies computer and information technologies—are important for economic development and attractive to students and scholars. I applaud these developments but worry that they will crowd out parts of the curriculum devoted to the study of the great humanistic traditions that have evolved in all civilizations throughout human history. Exposure to these traditions contributes to the formation of values and to an understanding of the richness and diversity of human experience.

The complexities of world problems and societies today require people educated in broad humanistic traditions in addition to the guidance and direction provided by the teaching of their religion. The history of the twentieth century is replete with examples of the danger of the systematic propagation and uncritical acceptance of dogmas, ideologies, and even theologies. More than ever, I believe that universities must shoulder the responsibility for helping build the capacity for moral judgment in complex settings. This is another area where the leading universities of the world can individually and collectively respond to a shared opportunity and a shared responsibility.

I will close by returning briefly to some basic themes. Higher education in the developing world operates under enormous pressures for which there are no simple solutions. Private institutions can make a contribution through experimentation and, where they are successful, as models. Linkages between institutions—particularly international linkages—are critical to this process.

The identification of new sources of finance for higher education has to be a high priority. National governments in the developing world are hard-pressed to meet existing education budgets, not to mention the additional funding required for expansion to accommodate growing populations, deal with a backlog of problems, and introduce new programs. International agencies, public and private, will help, but only within limits. It will be essential to identify private-sector funding and to create a regulatory environment that encourages private companies to support higher education.

It has been said that the Internet is the most important development for education since the invention of the printing press. Perhaps. But it is grossly underused for education, at least for now. Universities around the world should take on the task of developing educational materials, resources, and programs for the Internet. They should add their voices to critics of regulations and policies that impinge on the use of the World Wide Web for educational purposes in favor of commercial interests.

Let us remember the historic role of the university in the study, interpretation, and transmission of the great humanistic traditions of the world. Our search for global peace in an interconnected, crowded world with rising expectations needs to understand and internalize these lessons more than at any time in the past.

Thank you.

Your Highness, we thank you very much for your profound thoughts, for the actions that you have taken upon those thoughts, and for the challenges you have placed before us this evening.

—Charles M. Vest
President, Massachusetts
Institute of Technology

4

COMPETING DEMANDS
ON UNIVERSITIES

APRIL 23, 2001

Robert Berdahl is chancellor of the University of California, Berkeley and vice-chair of the Association of American Universities. After joining the history faculty at the University of Oregon, Dr. Berdahl served in the senior administration of the University of Oregon and at the University of Illinois at Urbana-Champaign. In 1993, he left Champaign for Austin to serve as president of the University of Texas at Austin. In 1997, he became chancellor at the University of California, Berkeley.

Dr. Berdahl is committed to undergraduate education and outreach to the community, especially primary and secondary schools.

—Charles M. Vest
President, Massachusetts
Institute of Technology

INTRODUCTION

Robert Berdahl

CHANCELLOR, UNIVERSITY OF CALIFORNIA, BERKELEY

F EW INSTITUTIONS IN OUR SOCIETIES HAVE AS MANY STAKEHOLDERS AS DO contemporary universities. Few institutions have as many competing groups, each claiming primary ownership of the institution. These elements may vary slightly from country to country or from one type of university to another, but the fact remains that the university faces an often bewildering set of demands, virtually all of which end up being concentrated on its leadership.

There are the demands of the faculty, who have a rightful claim to be the body that truly defines the university. There are the demands of students, whose claims of ownership at times can become excruciatingly difficult to navigate; of parents, who, at many of our institutions, pay much of the cost of their children's education; of alumni, who, unfortunately, often bring back to the university more nostalgia than anything else; of the business community, which expects the university to serve it as a source of employees and ideas; of government, from which most of us

> The fact remains that the university faces an often bewildering set of demands, virtually all of which end up being concentrated on its leadership.

receive the bulk of our resources; of taxpayers and the general public; and of the communities in which universities are located and with which they often clash.

The demands of these and other stakeholders often conflict. Navigating successfully among them can be difficult. Leading an institution through changes that will offend in some way nearly all of these groups presents a remarkable challenge to all of us.

It is clear that the environment in which we exist is changing rapidly and imposing its own set of competing demands. The rapid onset of technological change is altering how we do business, communicate, gather information, and, indeed, how we teach and conduct research. It produces its own research demands and requires policy decisions that are difficult to make, especially in the shrinking time frame in which we are called upon to make them.

The research needs of our faculty call for resources on a scale that even the richest universities among us have trouble accommodating. Because of limitations on resources, we have to make judgments about an agenda that is often difficult and contentious.

The cost of information and equipment—coupled with the fact that research requires collaboration in a setting that was not designed to provide it—may require us to change the competitive paradigm that often has guided us in the past.

As we heard from the panel yesterday, the free market economy, with its corresponding demand for knowledge-based industries, calls upon universities to be the handmaiden of industry in ways that leave little room for support for disciplines in the social sciences and the humanities. This creates conflicting demands between what we know is necessary for a healthy civil society and the demands that are put upon us by other elements in that society.

> The cost of information and equipment—coupled with the fact that research requires collaboration in a setting that was not designed to provide it—may require us to change the competitive paradigm that often has guided us in the past.

> The free market economy, with its corresponding demand for knowledge-based industries, calls upon universities to be the handmaiden of industry in ways that leave little room for support for disciplines in the social sciences and the humanities.

To discuss these and other matters, we have three distinguished university leaders from three different parts of the world: Professor Sir Alec Broers, vice-chancellor of Cambridge University; Dr. Juan Ramón de la Fuente, rector of the National Autonomous University of Mexico; and Dr. Shigehiko Hasumi, former president of the University of Tokyo.

Sir Alec Broers has extensive international experience in academia—and in the real world. He received a bachelor's of science degree in physics and electronics from Melbourne University, and B.A., Ph.D., and doctor of science degrees in electrical engineering from Cambridge. He worked for IBM in the United States for almost twenty years, was appointed an IBM fellow, and served on that company's corporate technical committee and science advisory committee.

When Sir Alec returned to Cambridge University in 1984, he was elected professor of electrical engineering, fellow of Trinity College, master of Churchill College, and head of the university engineering department.

Sir Alec has served on many British government, European Economic Community, and NATO committees, including the U.K. Engineering and Physics Science and Research Council and the NATO Special Panel on Nanoscience. He has been recognized all over the world for his accomplishments. The American Institute of Physics, for example, awarded him its prize for industry applications of science. He is a fellow of the Royal Society, the Royal Academy of Engineering, the Institute of Electrical and Electronics Engineers, and the Institute of Physics, and a foreign associate of the U.S. National Academy of Engineering. He was knighted in 1998.

—Charles M. Vest
President, Massachusetts
Institute of Technology

THE BRITISH EXAMPLE

Sir Alec N. Broers
VICE-CHANCELLOR, UNIVERSITY OF CAMBRIDGE

THANK YOU, CHANCELLOR BERDAHL, AND THANK YOU ALL FOR inviting me here. It is a great privilege to be asked to participate in this meeting. I would particularly like to thank Chuck Vest, who has become a close colleague and friend through my university's collaboration with MIT.

I was somewhat at a loss as to what I would talk about at this meeting until I received an excellent letter from your president, Nils Hasselmo, which suggested that I should first talk about my three most serious challenges and then answer a series of questions.

So what are my three major challenges?

The first is the broad challenge that we all face: to provide the resources, incentives, and rewards necessary to attract and support world-class staff and students—in other words, to ensure that everyone in the university has the opportunity to reach his or her full potential.

You could say that about a lot of organizations, but it is particularly important in universities. We don't want our faculty held back by a lack of resources or not attracted to the university in the first place because of poor personal reward. At Cambridge, we must do this despite the fact that we receive our core funding on the same basis as the hundred-plus other universities in the United Kingdom.

So, the provision of competitive resources—especially how much we can pay people—is a real challenge for British universities. Members of AAU are in a much better position to pay people adequately than we are in Britain.

The problem is not so serious when it comes to research facilities. For example, over the last few years, through special programs from the government and money raised in the private and industrial sectors, we have gathered into Cambridge about a billion dollars for buildings, libraries, and equipment.

We must have a flexible organizational structure that can change easily. Academics find this idea alien. They feel that there must be one correct organizational structure, and they resist change.

The second challenge is to put in place an academic and administrative structure that can react rapidly and take best advantage of the information and communications revolution. We must have a flexible organizational structure that can change easily. Academics find this idea alien. They feel that there must be one correct organizational structure, and they resist change.

I spent twenty years in industry, where it wasn't unusual to reorganize every two or three years. This may not be appropriate for universities but the information, technology, and communications revolution requires us to be more flexible than we have been in the past.

My third challenge is to sustain the balance between the arts and humanities and the sciences and technologies. Cambridge is balanced in terms of the numbers of faculty and students, but naturally there is much more money for research in the sciences and technologies.

We have recently launched in Cambridge a new initiative, the Center for Research in the Social Sciences and Humanities, to restore this balance. I feel strongly that it is the balance among the cultures that is attractive to the most creative and innovative minds.

Now I will answer the questions that Nils Hasselmo posed.

How are the academic programs and facilities at Cambridge supported?
The Higher Education Funding Council of England provides about one-third of the overall funding for the leading universities and about two-thirds for those further down the scale. At Cambridge, the rest comes from a wide spectrum of resources: 13 percent from government research councils,

19 percent from nongovernment research sources, 7 percent from home fees (fees paid by British students), 6 percent from overseas fees, and 11.5 percent from endowment income.

If we wanted to replace government funding with endowment, we would need to raise about $3 billion—an unrealistic goal. Although people talk about the possible privatization of some of the leading universities in the United Kingdom, I do not think that is feasible. Besides, the majority of academics would not want it—most of them want to be part of a national, integrated higher education system.

We are in the process of carrying out an interesting exercise for the Treasury called "the transparency review," in which we are required to show in some detail how our academics spend their time and money. That's a challenge if ever you had one. Everybody must determine how much time they spend on research and how much on teaching. The purpose is to discover whether the money allocated for teaching is in fact being spent on teaching and not subsidizing research, and vice versa.

Although the full report is not yet out, it has become clear that both teaching and research are being subsidized, in effect, by universities' own resources. The major subsidy comes from academics' unpaid overtime. Most academics are working 50 to 60 hours a week, and not the 40 hours that the government thinks they are working. The rest of the subsidy is in the form of private university funds. The full results of the report will appear toward the end of the year.

What does the British public expect of the university?
The public's perception, to the extent that it is known, is that universities provide, using government funds, an excellent higher education for students from all backgrounds and abilities. However, many people think that students should be able to contribute immediately to their work environment on graduation. I mention this to highlight a problem: that there is insufficient willingness on the part of business and industry to train people.

We do not intend in a university like Cambridge to train graduates so that they can fully function in a specialist job immediately on

We do not intend in a university like Cambridge to train graduates so that they can fully function in a specialist job immediately on graduation. We teach students to think and to learn. Specialist knowledge must be obtained on the job.

graduation. We teach students to think and to learn. Specialist knowledge must be obtained on the job.

The public expects that universities will be major providers of high-quality employment in their local regions. I hope we do that. But universities also provide a community of scholars and experts that can advise society and government on cultural and scientific matters.

Of Cambridge there are additional expectations: that the ancient buildings will be immaculately maintained; that the music in the college chapels will be at a standard unequalled in the world; and that the boat race will provide entertainment, through the excellence of the oarsmen, for a worldwide audience of 200 million people.

How is the research agenda set at Cambridge?
Research projects are initiated almost entirely by individual academics or by groups of academics. The governing body of the university is the Regent House, the entire group of roughly 3,000 academics. If the Council of the university, which is the senior administrative committee, makes a decision about something that it feels should change, the proposal for change has to published and the Regent House given the opportunity to discuss and approve it. Any 10 of those 3,000 academics can call for a referendum. So it is the individual members of the faculty who determine what is done.

The majority of the funding for high-capital-cost science and technology projects comes from industry, the research councils, the British government, the European Community, and charities. (Charities are very significant in Britain because of the Wellcome Trust, one of the largest charities in the world.) The funding is generally acquired and administered by individual principal investigators. There's very little top-down direction of research at Cambridge.

Do political changes in the British government affect Cambridge's agenda?
Although the funding councils provide only about a third of the overall funding of leading universities, the government claims the right to monitor all of the spending. It does not interfere directly in the way we run the universities, but it can exert considerable influence over the agenda of the funding councils and encourage its own initiatives.

Would a change of government make any difference? It certainly would. For example, the Conservative Party has proposed a scheme that would allow some of the leading universities to privatize by endowing them rather than having them receive recurrent funding. The problem with this scheme is that there is a large difference between the amount of money the universities estimate is necessary and the amount that would be available from the public purse.

> The Conservative Party has proposed a scheme that would allow some of the leading universities to privatize by endowing them rather than having them receive recurrent funding.

How do we evaluate our faculty members' performance as teachers and researchers?
The teaching of individual academics is assessed within the university by ongoing, informal peer review and regular student assessment. But the bigger and perhaps the strongest influence is informal peer review. It is generally known via the tutorial system whose lectures are good and popular, and whose students do well in exams and whose do not.

In Cambridge, we evaluate the performance of departments and faculties on a six-year cycle. The General Board of the Faculties, the senior academic committee, appoints a review committee, which reports its findings back to the board. If that review reveals weaknesses, then a committee with external members is appointed to carry out a more comprehensive review.

This process has worked well in Cambridge for decades. However, there is now an added government-driven process, also on a six-year cycle, that assesses the quality of teaching in individual subjects. There is also an evaluation of the research performance of an institution, referred to as the research assessment exercise, which I will come to in a moment.

The assessments of teaching quality are intensive, and bureaucratic, and rely on the evaluation of the process as much as output. They have not been popular among universities because of the heavy bureaucratic load they impose. It can take six months of intense effort to prepare for an assessment. A large room has to be set aside for the reams of paper that are needed to supply background data.

As a result of pressure from the university sector, the British secretary of state recently promised that a lighter touch would be applied, for which we all had been arguing. "Units of assessment," as they are called, that receive more than twenty points out of twenty-four will miss one round of assessment. I'm pleased to say that includes every department in Cambridge that has been assessed under the current process.

Research performance of individual academics is assessed formally as part of the research assessment exercise. This is something that has been more willingly accepted by British academics than the assessment of the quality of teaching. The process has been carefully honed. I think we would still rather be without it, but it works better than the teaching quality assessment.

How does Cambridge compete and collaborate with sister institutions?
At present, there's no competition for general teaching funds among British universities. The teaching quality exercise is not reflected in funding, although there are some small competitive initiatives, mainly to do with access. When it comes to research, however, the grant from government depends strongly on the research assessment exercise.

Many of the research council– and charity-funded initiatives encourage and reward collaboration, so there is a lot of research collaboration between universities in the United Kingdom. British universities work together successfully for industry, government, and other entities.

What role does international competition and collaboration among universities play?
We have international collaborations between Cambridge and many universities throughout the world—generally organized by individual academics. The collaborations are important because they keep communications open and offer the possibility for further collaboration. But they are on a relatively small scale.

We have one large-scale collaboration, and that is with MIT. It is funded with approximately $100 million from the British government and from British industry. Its intent is to enhance the financial competitiveness of the United Kingdom.

The Cambridge-MIT Institute, CMI, has been established to direct the collaboration. CMI is conducting four programs. The first is an exchange of undergraduates. In the coming year, we intend to have about twenty-five third-year undergraduates coming to Cambridge from MIT and twenty-five going to MIT from Cambridge. The second is the establishment of professional practice courses, such as specialized master's courses in the management of technology. The third is collaborative research. By combining our research expertise, Cambridge will participate in the U.S. research community and MIT in the European research community. And fourth, a new National Competitive Network will provide information about CMI programs to other U.K. universities.

The collaboration is now underway. Extensive legal agreements had to be drawn up between each university and CMI, and between CMI and the government, but they have been completed and the collaboration is generating excitement in both institutions.

In finishing, I would like to say to this audience that we in Cambridge are committed to keeping our university among the leading universities in the world, such as yours. We believe that we will be able to do this only by being a closely integrated member of the international community.

Thank you very much, indeed, for inviting me to speak this morning.

Dr. Juan Ramón de la Fuente is rector of the National Autonomous University of Mexico, a prominent physician, scholar, and health care reformer. Dr. de la Fuente graduated from the medical school of the Autonomous University, where he is currently a professor of psychiatry, and did postgraduate work at the Mayo Clinic in Rochester.

At the Autonomous University he served as director of clinical research, vice-chancellor of science, and dean of the medical school. After being appointed secretary of health by the president of Mexico, he directed an ambitious reform of the country's health care system.

He has published more than 250 papers and thirteen books and has lectured widely around the world. He has served as vice president of the World Health Assembly in Geneva, chaired the United Nations AIDS program, and is currently a member of the board of directors of the International Association of Universities.

Dr. de la Fuente has been widely recognized for his contributions. Several medical societies and institutions have named him an honorary fellow and awarded him their doctorate. He is a former president of the Mexican Academy of Sciences and president-elect of the National Academy of Medicine in Mexico. He has received prizes and awards, including those from the National Academy of Medicine, the Academy of Scientific Research, the Mexican chapter of the American College of Physicians, and the Mayo Foundation.

—Charles M. Vest
President, Massachusetts
Institute of Technology

THE PERSPECTIVE FROM MEXICO

Juan Ramón de la Fuente

RECTOR, NATIONAL AUTONOMOUS UNIVERSITY OF MEXICO

I WANT TO THANK YOU FOR YOUR KIND INVITATION AND THE OPPORTUNITY you've given me today to share some reflections. It is appropriate for us to be in Washington now as a new relationship develops between presidents Fox and Bush.

My first academic appointment was at the University of Minnesota. That was quite a few years ago, when Nils Hasselmo was the president of the university. This occasion has allowed me to get back in touch with him and with the association.

I would like to discuss some of the points that are influencing most directly the competing demands on Mexican universities. The first set of factors has to do with the economy.

The degree of openness in the Mexican economy has increased tremendously since the North American Free Trade Agreement (NAFTA) was signed in 1994. Exports rose from just 20 percent of Mexico's GDP in 1983 to 60 percent in 1999.

The composition of exports in the Mexican economy also has changed. In 1985 Mexican exports were dominated by oil and oil-related products, but by 1999 most of our exports were manufactured goods (figure 1). Over that period, Mexican manufacturing exports increased more than twenty-fold. The resulting transformation of the economy created new demands on higher education.

Mexico has become the second largest trading partner of the United States, after Canada. Mexico's exports to the U.S. market have consistently increased more than those of the rest of the world, and certainly more than those from the rest of Latin America—a trend that is expected to continue (figure 2).

Because of the high degree of integration between Mexico and its North American partners—the United States and Canada—there is a need to integrate academic institutions in the region. But trade agreements, particularly NAFTA, have moved ahead much more rapidly than have cooperative efforts between such institutions as universities, and other academic and cultural enterprises.

The need for cooperation will become even more important with the signing—April 22 in Quebec City—of the protocol for the Latin American Free Trade Agreement, which will bring together all of the countries in the hemisphere. If things happen as they have with NAFTA, trade and commerce will move quickly. North American universities need to move much faster than we have so far.

Free trade is now a worldwide reality. I was surprised to hear one of the members of the staff of President Bush say that for the United States, NAFTA

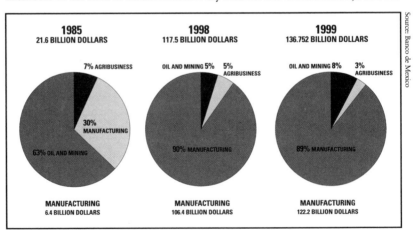

Figure 1. Composition of Mexico's exports, by sector, 1985, 1998, and 1999

has represented an increase in exports of between $40 billion and $60 billion a year. If that is true, the benefits to the U.S. of free trade are amazing.

The Mexican economy has become integrated with the rest of the world in more than just trade. Mexico is now one of the main recipients of direct foreign investment, second only to China. This poses a challenge for academic institutions in Mexico because we must produce the professionals needed to supply high-quality services to the new industries established in Mexico.

An important effect of NAFTA has been to provoke the deregulation of secondary systems that block the efficient flow of information, goods, and services. But we are way behind in loosening existing rules and regulations governing human resources. For example, an appendix to the NAFTA agreement contains a long list specifying the positions for which an individual must possess a secondary school diploma, postsecondary diploma, state license, local license, and so on. It is not just lawyers or other professionals who must meet specific certification requirements, but also technicians and technologists working in the sciences.

This red tape gets in our way. We need single instruments that will assess people's competence and abilities. If those requirements are met, that should be it. Otherwise, our university faculty, students, and other profes-

> Trade agreements, have moved ahead much more rapidly than have cooperative efforts between such institutions as universities, and other academic and cultural enterprises.

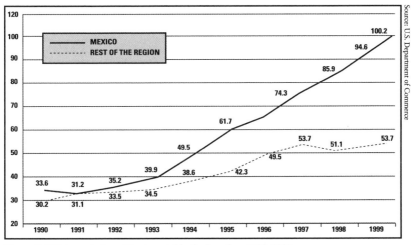

Figure 2. U.S. imports from Mexico and Latin America, 1990–1999

Source: U.S. Department of Commerce

sionals are not going to interact at the same rate as the rest of our economies.

We talked yesterday about brain drain. One of the less-discussed but important factors in the brain drain is the high certification requirements that individuals must meet before they can participate in the U.S. and Canadian economies. By the time people complete the process, returning home may not seem worthwhile; they have already accomplished 50 percent of what they expected to accomplish in their lifetime.

Groups are looking at these issues, but the human resource problems have not been looked at systematically.

A common concern seems to be the humanities, the arts, and the social sciences. These disciplines are connected to economic issues in the sense that one sees little demand for them in the market, including the labor market. As a result, they have low priority at the university. In Mexico, as in most other Latin American countries, we are having difficulty funding the humanities, some of the social sciences, and the arts.

> Globalization means partnership and working together. It is not enough to know one's technical subject well—people need skills that will allow them to interact effectively and appropriately across cultures.

But these disciplines are necessary for dealing appropriately with global issues. Not only do they play an important role in sustaining national identity, but they are key to dealing with the many intercultural processes in which we are involved.

My last point is that we need to review the agenda for collaboration between and among universities and introduce some points that have not been taken into consideration.

Among the lessons of globalization is that we need to pay more attention to the cultural aspects of competence. Globalization means partnership and working together. It is not enough to know one's technical subject well—people need skills that will allow them to interact effectively and appropriately across cultures.

We must ask ourselves if we are teaching our students to have "intercultural competence": to work well in multicultural teams, to speak other languages, to adjust to new environments, and to deal effectively with ethnic diversity.

We need more structured programs of education and training in intercultural competence, programs that should include the role of international students. Student exchanges were once very important between Mexico and our neighbors to the north, but in recent years they have slowed. We need to look at student exchanges again, but this time from the perspective of international students as a cross-cultural resource for domestic students. We must better identify how domestic students benefit from student exchanges and not focus solely on how the exchange students, themselves, benefit.

Another issue we should look at is the academic mobility of faculty. Have we developed an international faculty? Is it needed?

Finally, I think it would be appropriate for our meeting to end with this idea: We need to educate our students—and ourselves—to become better global participants, better able to understand other people on their own terms, and more appreciative of our own heritages. Intercultural experiences, aided by the development of intercultural competence, offer such a promise.

We need to look at student exchanges again, but this time from the perspective of international students as a cross-cultural resource for domestic students.

I have reviewed with you some of the aspects that impose new, competing demands on universities, along with other problems we must face in becoming an international, global society. What happened yesterday in Quebec City is very important. It means that in four years we should have a free trade agreement among all the countries of this continent. We should try to take advantage of it.

I thank you very much again for your hospitality and the opportunity you've given me to share these thoughts with you this morning. Thank you.

*Shigehiko Hasumi served as president of the
University of Tokyo until March 2001. His scholarship and academic experience cross many international lines.*

*After receiving his B.A. and M.A. degrees in
French literature from the University of Tokyo, Dr.
Hasumi studied at the University of Paris, where he
received his doctorate.*

*At the University of Tokyo, he has been a pro-
fessor and dean in the faculty of arts and sciences. In
1995, he became vice-president of the university and
in 1997 was appointed president.*

*During his career, Dr. Hasumi has lectured in
many forums around the world, chaired and participated in a variety of international symposia, and
supervised students from many countries in the fields
of French literature, film history, and the theory of
criticism.*

*Dr. Hasumi, like our other panelists, also has a
distinguished record of affiliation with various organizations. He chaired the Association of Japanese
National Universities and the Association of East
Asian Research Universities, and, as a prominent film
critic, has served on juries for the Locarno and other
international film festivals.*

*His books cover a remarkable range of subjects
and have received many awards, including those from
the Japanese Ministry of Education, the French Film
Critics Association, and the Omiyuri Literature Prize.
In 1999, he was named a Commandeur des Arts et
des Lettres, the highest award from the French government for art and culture.*

*—Charles M. Vest
President, Massachusetts
Institute of Technology*

ESCAPING FROM THE JAPANESE MODEL

Shigehiko Hasumi
PRESIDENT EMERITUS, UNIVERSITY OF TOKYO

I n this year of 2001, a time that symbolizes so many changes, I was pleased to be given the unexpected opportunity to speak here in Washington, D.C. I would like to thank President Hasselmo and all of the members of AAU for this great honor. Please allow me to extend my sincere congratulations to the AAU on the celebration of its centennial last year.

Before I begin, I would like first to inform you that Professor Sasaki, former dean of the School of Law, has been selected as the twenty-seventh president of the University of Tokyo. He assumed his new post on April 1. That date also happens to mark the start of the academic year in Japan.

The president of the University of Tokyo is elected by the entire faculty to a four-year term. This tradition dates back to 1919 and survived even the meddling of Japan's military government during World War II. In one election about a decade ago, the two final candidates each received exactly the same number of votes, so in accordance with our rules, the winner had to be chosen by lot. But President Sasaki's election, I am happy to report, proceeded smoothly, with none of the confusion that occurred recently in Florida.

With the completion of my own term as our university's president, I also resigned my post as president of the Association of National Universities of Japan. Chosen as my successor was Professor Nagao, the president of Kyoto University. It would seem more proper for either President Sasaki or President Nagao to be giving this speech, but the honor has fallen to me instead, thanks to the urging of the organizers of this meeting, Charles Vest of MIT and Steven Sample of the University of Southern California. I am very fortunate for the irreplaceable friendships that I have formed with them through our joint international projects and am deeply grateful for their kind invitation.

For the past two years, I also served as chairman of the Association of East Asian Research Universities. It is a great pleasure to meet here again many of the members of that association: President Zhihong Xu of Peking University, who spoke yesterday; Presidents Sasaki and Nagao, whom I just mentioned; Tadamitsu Kishimoto, the president of Osaka University; Ki-Jun Lee, the president of Seoul National University; and Wei-Jao Chen, who is both president of Taiwan National University and vice-chairman of the association.

The Association of East Asian Universities was established in 1996 and now has seventeen member institutions in China, Hong Kong, Japan, Korea, and Taiwan. It sponsors a dozen workshops on topics ranging from molecular biology and biotechnology to Asian culture and holds student camps twice a year at member universities.

The relations between universities in East Asia are much more active than they were a decade ago. Last year, President Xu of Peking University and I organized a meeting of Chinese and Japanese university presidents in Tokyo. The ties between Seoul National University and the University of Tokyo have also become closer, and this past March, President Lee of Seoul National came to Tokyo and gave a memorable speech at our graduation ceremony.

These lively contacts have extended beyond the university presidents to include many scholars and graduate students. Exchanges of undergraduates, however, remain inadequate. Registration fees and tuition are quite expensive in Japan, and discussions between governments about resolving these issues have made little progress.

Nevertheless, in 1995, the University of Tokyo still was able to start a short-term exchange program for undergraduate students, based on rather complex interuniversity agreements for credit transfers. All of the classes are conducted in English. The program has been well received and a valuable step toward allowing undergraduates to move more freely among universities in neighboring countries.

Because universities in East Asia have great differences in their histories and structures, it is difficult to make generalizations about them. If the leading universities in our region share one similarity, it is that most of them were established about a hundred years ago. Kyoto University celebrated its 100th anniversary in 1997, and Peking University in 1998. In a few days, Tsinghua University in Beijing will mark its ninetieth anniversary, and Osaka University its seventieth anniversary in two weeks. Taiwan National University had its seventieth anniversary celebration in 1998, and Chulalongkorn University marked its eighty-fourth anniversary in March.

The oldest modern university in East Asia, the University of Tokyo, was born in 1877, nine years after the University of California, Berkeley and three years before the University of Southern California. When it was founded, the University of Tokyo consisted of faculties of law, science, literature, and medicine. Later, faculties of engineering, agriculture, and economics were added.

> The major universities in East Asia were established at the high point of imperialism. Japan was then implementing modernization programs modeled on the European system and regarded higher education as one of the necessary institutions of the state.

At that time in the United States, nationwide professional organizations were being set up, including the American Historical Association and the American Physical Society. I learned these facts from a speech that Chancellor Berdahl gave at a forum of university presidents three years ago in Beijing, a speech later published by Peking University Press in a volume entitled The University of the Twenty-first Century. At the turn of the last century in Japan, there were only two imperial universities, in Tokyo and Kyoto.

In her book, *The Origins of Totalitarianism*, Hannah Arendt referred to the three decades from 1884 to 1914 in Europe as the "age of imperialism." Whether or not one accepts her time divisions, it is certainly true that the major universities in East Asia were established at the high point of imperialism. Japan was then implementing modernization programs modeled on the European system and regarded higher education as one of the necessary institutions of the state. At the time, Karl Marx, exiled from Germany, was writing *Das Kapital* in the reading room of the British Museum in Victorian London. Although the gigantic steel tower that would immortalize the name of Gustave Eiffel had not yet been built in Paris, the symbol of the Second Empire, the Théâtre National de l'Opéra, had just been completed.

I refer to institutions of higher learning that were reorganized in Europe when capitalism was entering the imperialistic stage by the term "second-generation" universities. In contrast, the "first generation" universities, which emerged in the Middle Ages in Europe, had evolved slowly through the Renaissance and into the seventeenth and eighteenth centuries.

Those first-generation universities were fundamentally different from the universities of the nineteenth century. Their scholarship was based on transcendental concepts of theology and metaphysics that would be of little use to the ambitious, utilitarian classes that began to form in the cities with the arrival of the Industrial Revolution. The industrial progress of the nation-state required greater focus on worldly values, and achieving those values required the widespread acquisition of practical skills. The financial responsibility for that progress was to be borne by the state.

The East Asian institutions of higher learning established a century ago adopted the practical utilitarianism of the European second-generation universities in a somewhat exaggerated form. They were promoted as part of national policies to build the infrastructure of a modern society—infrastructure that also included roads, railways, train stations, bridges, government offices, hospitals, and factories. No fundamental distinction was made between universities and these other endeavors. The University of Tokyo was one of the first schools to take seriously the fields of engineering and agriculture, which were still not regarded as real sciences in Europe. Thus, from the very beginning, the university in Japan, closely linked to industry, was under the indirect control of the state.

This situation had three consequences. The first was that Japanese universities had no interest in metaphysics, because they had no institutional memory of the transcendental concepts that had been the foundation of the first-generation universities. Laws were not regarded in Japan as embodiments of universal justice. Instead, in a caricature of Kant's version of the Copernican Revolution, something was considered just if it was written in the laws.

The second consequence was that, like Plato's shoemakers who made only shoes, scholars would lock themselves up in narrow research specialties with no sense of the universality of science. Such specialization created a gap that is still difficult to close between basic research, which aims to create shared knowledge, and applied research, which is linked to proprietary interests.

> Like Plato's shoemakers who made only shoes, scholars would lock themselves up in narrow research specialties with no sense of the universality of science.

The third consequence was the appearance of the abstract notion of "academic freedom"—set in opposition to utilitarian research goals. That notion played a positive role during the war period. But some researchers took it as an excuse to close themselves off in their exclusive little domains. That isolation, which is symbolized by the ugly clock towers that still dominate many university campuses in Japan, gave academics a sterile sense of superiority. In any case, universities in Japan functioned throughout the twentieth century only as institutions of the nation-state and lacked any significant international perspective.

When I took office as the president of University of Tokyo four years ago, I saw that Japanese universities would have no future if they tried to extend their accomplishments only within the framework of second-generation universities. That is why I proposed the concept of the "third-generation" university. One of the ideals I advocated was to break out of the nation-state framework left over from the nineteenth century. As one step in that direction, I set the goal of eliminating from our university discrimination based on gender, nationality, and age.

In the area of gender, a ridiculous situation had taken root in many departments, especially in the sciences and engineering, where research opportunities existed solely for Japanese men. To change that unfortunate tradition, I gave the departments funding for an extra assistant whenever a female professor was hired. When it was impossible to promote accomplished women because of the lack of open posts, I arranged temporary professorial posts for women.

Although these efforts have not yet yielded adequate results, a significant number of women have become faculty members in the humanities, and leading positions on the president's staff are now held by women from both the humanities and sciences.

With regard to nationality, the law was revised in the 1980s to allow non-Japanese citizens to be hired as civil servants in education. The University of Tokyo now has on its faculty an American teaching Japanese literature in English and in Japanese, a French woman teaching the Chinese language in Japanese, an American man teaching Korean culture in both Korean and English, a Belgian man teaching Japanese theater in Japanese and French, and a Chinese-American teaching legal philosophy in Japanese and English. Our foreign faculty continues to grow, and I expect the trend to accelerate in our science and engineering departments as well.

During my term, I confronted the age issue by raising the retirement age from sixty to sixty-five. Because of Japan's economic slump, reaction to that move was very negative, but I insisted on it for three reasons. First of all, the retirement age had been set at sixty in the 1920s when the average life span was less than sixty. I did not believe such a rule was appropriate for the twenty-first century. It was unproductive for our best scholars to leave the university at age sixty and spend the rest of their lives at private universities or unemployed.

The case of Dr. Hideki Shirakawa, who won the Nobel Prize in Chemistry last year, exemplifies the problem. Dr. Shirakawa had been a professor at the National University of Tsukuba, but because he had passed the retirement age, he was no longer working there when he won the prize. Of the three people who won the prize simultaneously, he was the only one who was officially unemployed.

My second reason for raising the retirement age was that mandatory retirement at age sixty made it difficult to recruit leading scholars over fifty from Japan or other countries. Soon after we decided to raise the retirement age, we were fortunate to hire an outstanding forty-five-year-old professor from the United States.

The third reason for raising the retirement age was that I had observed a tendency for many scholars to move away from research in their mid-fifties because they expected to retire at sixty.

Most of our departments accepted my proposal and adopted term appointment systems with strict guidelines for evaluating professional accomplishments. I am confident that these changes will bring new vitality to our university.

Even if we open offices for technology transfer between universities and industry and make it easier for the university to receive funding from private corporations; even if we lay the infrastructure for electronic communications around our campuses and build full-scale facilities for distance learning; even if we sign agreement after agreement for exchanging researchers and students with foreign universities, as long as there is no significant reform in gender, nationality, and age, Japanese universities will be unable to break free of the shackles that have made them institutions of Japanese, for Japanese, and by Japanese.

> As long as there is no significant reform in gender, nationality, and age, Japanese universities will be unable to break free of the shackles that have made them institutions of Japanese, for Japanese, and by Japanese.

The Japanese government is now implementing major cuts in the civil service, including employees of national universities. While this is a serious issue, even more serious is a government plan to transfer some of the work of ministries to "independent administrative institutions" in order to improve the government's finances. Tax collection and immigration are among the functions envisioned for the new entities, which would be required to meet numerical targets. A law governing their operation has passed the Diet.

National museums, which already have become independent administrative institutions, must now establish targets for visitors in the next fiscal year. Their budgets are then based on those targets. This quantification of cultural activities without regard to their quality is a barbaric bureaucratic measure.

We worry that the national universities may soon be confronting a similar barbarism, for it is now being debated whether or not the universities also should become independent administrative institutions. If the government forces such administrative reform onto the Japanese universities while still having no higher education policy for the next century, it will be very difficult to improve the quality of education and research.

Japan invests only 0.6 percent of its GDP in higher education—much less than Europe and North America. In spite of this low investment, our government insists that universities raise funds from the private sector. Of course, the University of Tokyo benefits from important joint financing projects. But it is unimaginable that private industry, for example, would invest in a gigantic experimental facility for high-energy particle physics.

Gerhard Casper, former president of Stanford, made an important statement three years ago in Beijing:

> We also have to keep in mind that support from industry can be of great significance, but, in light of expenses involved, will not supplant research funding from the state. Basic research is a public good that business, given its orientation towards profit, can produce only in a limited quantity on its own. This is an insight governments tend to forget all too frequently, especially in time of fiscal crisis.

Unfortunately, Casper's statement applies to the current Japanese government.

Perhaps I have overemphasized some of the negative aspects of our topic. In fact, I am not pessimistic about the future of our universities. What gives me hope is that, despite financial neglect, the University of Tokyo has, through its own efforts, been able to maintain its research and education at an international level.

Although Japan is now said to be in a serious economic recession, our society is seeking changes that are more sound than during the boom times of the 1980s, when the Japanese model was being trumpeted as victorious.

Now, for the first time in our modern history, individual Japanese have begun to think and act for themselves, regardless of their status within their organizations. The old Japanese model was an ugly monument to the age when our politicians, bureaucrats, businesspeople, and even academics failed to take responsibility for analyzing their situations, proposing visions for the future, and implementing change. Fearing change, they clung to the belief that the nineteenth century nation-state must be preserved at all costs.

The age is coming to an end when people were protected by large organizations and could expect to receive their due allocations of happiness as long as they did their work. I welcome the collapse of that old system and believe that the change bodes well for Japan's future. When the transformations in our society pick up speed and become focused effectively, the third-generation university will truly begin to function in Japan.

The age is coming to an end when people were protected by large organizations and could expect to receive their due allocations of happiness as long as they did their work.

S E S S I O N   D I S C U S S I O N

MR. BERDAHL: I want to thank our panelists for three very interesting and enlightening presentations about the circumstances affecting institutions in their countries. Thanks to Alec Broers for discussing funding, structure, and international initiatives at Cambridge; to Juan Ramón de la Fuente for showing how economic change and free trade in the western hemisphere are creating new opportunities and new imperatives for Mexican universities; and to Shigehiko Hasumi for his very interesting history of Japanese universities as part of the public infrastructure of modernization in Japan. I particularly appreciate his presentation about the changes he has led with respect to nationality, gender, and age.

I'm sure these have prompted many questions and responses from our audience here today. I'll open the floor for questions.

DON MICHAEL RANDEL, President, University of Chicago: President Hasumi has very nicely made explicit a theme that has been running through our discussion: that the modern university, as we know it, is essentially a product of the nation-state and has existed to serve the purposes of the nation-state. What we confront now with globalization is the weakening of the role of the nation-state.

How then are we to rethink universities in light of that fact? Who will be the master of the university, its animating presence? How do we resolve the continuing need for public and governmental support of universities with this decline in the place of the nation-state in the modern economy? In particular, as we lament the lack of support for the humanities and social sciences, how do we deal with the fact that their place in the modern university was to educate citizens, and that with the decline of the nation-state, the need to educate citizens of particular states also tends to decline?

MR. BERDAHL: Several of our speakers have addressed the need to educate citizens of the world, but let me turn to the panel. Who would like to respond first? President Hasumi?

MR. HASUMI: It is true that the concept of the nation-state is disappearing, but I think support from the government is absolutely necessary to the governance of the university. Private companies could finance the university, but unfortunately, their interest is only in the applied sciences. We must educate society to see that the role of the university is not limited to the promotion of applied sciences. Our goal is the promotion of scholarship in general, including basic sciences, social sciences, and the humanities.

Yesterday we discussed whether or not education is important in research universities. But the dangerous distinction now being made in society, at least in Japan, is not the distinction between research and education. It is the focus on training over learning, between professional training and learning in the real sense of the word. I am very pessimistic about this because Japanese society has asked the university to do far more professional training than broad education.

> The dangerous distinction now being made in society, at least in Japan, is not the distinction between research and education. It is the focus on training over learning, between professional training and learning in the real sense of the word.

MR. BERDAHL: Juan Ramón de la Fuente?

MR. DE LA FUENTE: The question, from my perspective, is whether or not universities will succumb to market forces. If it is going to happen, we need to look at some other type of regional organization—or reorganization—for postsecondary education. My personal view is that we shouldn't allow universities to succumb completely to market forces, no matter how important the market is these days.

MR. BROERS: I'd just make a quick point here. We have a particular problem with science funding from charities in the United Kingdom because they do not believe in paying overhead. This removes the financial margin that we need if we are to implement our own priorities and sustain the breadth of our cultures.

In practice, the charities do not pay overhead and even may require the university to supplement their funding. They will give an investigator £700,000 and tell the individual to find the other £300,000. The process works because the charities have never found an academic who won't take £700,000 when it is offered.

The universities then have to scramble to find the rest of the money, which must come from discretionary funds that otherwise would be used for balancing support between the sciences and the arts and humanities.

LARRY FAULKNER, President, University of Texas at Austin: I have a question for Juan Ramón de la Fuente. Juan Ramón, you talked about the coupling of the university to changes in the trade environment and made the point that you didn't feel the universities had kept up with what had evolved from NAFTA. I wonder if you could be more specific about that?

MR. DE LA FUENTE: Thank you, Larry. Yes, indeed, if we look at the changes that have occurred in regional economy and trade, and then look at regional interactions in culture, science, and academia during the same span of time, we lag behind. We haven't made much progress in getting rid of the red tape. That was the very first thing that people did in trade: they sat down and said, "What are the obstacles to free trade? What's coming between us?" They removed barriers that had been in place for years, often from sheer inertia.

We in the university community have not done that. Perhaps AAU and its counterpart, the Association of Mexican Universities, could look at this issue more specifically. They could ask, "What could we do to simplify our relationship?"

We basically have the same relationship that we've had for the past twenty or thirty years, based on the interests of individual colleagues, friends, and groups that have worked together. Those relationships are fine, and we don't want to interfere with them by bringing in the university bureaucracy. But what are the real possibilities these days for mobility of undergraduate students? As our neighbor, the University of Texas has had a very important relationship with Mexican universities for many years. Yet how many Mexican students are at Austin doing some sort of educational program or exchange? How many students from the University of Texas at Austin do we have in Mexican universities? The answer is very few. There's not a single program for that.

The point is that we have not brought this issue into our bilateral agenda or into our trilateral agenda with Canada. In the face of the Latin American Free Trade Agreement, it is time to look at it more seriously.

> The University of Texas has had a very important relationship with Mexican universities for many years. Yet how many Mexican students are at Austin doing some sort of educational program or exchange? How many students from the University of Texas at Austin do we have in Mexican universities? The answer is very few.

JURGEN MLYNEK, President, Humboldt University of Berlin: Sir Alec mentioned three challenges. One was finding flexible structures inside the university—different, I assume, from departments and faculties. I also assume that the idea is to find appropriate frames for interdisciplinary research and teaching.

Could you elaborate on that? How can we go from static to more dynamic units that can be born and then die?

MR. BROERS: What I propose is quite down-to-earth and pragmatic. We have traditionally managed the university through a large number of committees, many of which have been in existence for a long time. They are written into our statutes and ordinances. We have been trying to get away from this fixed structure and operate with working groups that will come together for a while to work on specific topics.

The members of these groups can be chosen to suit the topic. For example, we need specialists for e-university projects.

That's all I mean. It's nothing terribly sophisticated. The working groups should have a finite life and be disbanded when the desired decisions have been made. Naturally, in an academic community, the decisions are made in a democratic manner, so I am not talking about a hierarchical management system.

The nation-state may be declining, but nationalism is not. Many of the issues—access versus excellence, training versus education, science and medicine versus humanities—relate to nationalism.

ALBERT CARNESALE, Chancellor, University of California, Los Angeles: I have a question and a comment. None of you mentioned primary and secondary education as a source of demands on your university, and yet in the United States we face increasing demands from this quarter. The United States is viewed as having excellent universities, but poor education below that. People look to the universities to fix the problem. I wonder if you'd comment on that.

My own comment is as follows. You have been talking about the decline of the nation-state, but many of the demands that you are focusing on actually are indications of the rise of nationalism. The nation-state may be declining, but nationalism is not. Many of the issues—access versus excellence, training versus education, science and medicine versus humanities—

relate to nationalism. In the United States we have an organization called the Council on Competitiveness, of which many AAU institutions are members. People pretend to forget where the title came from, but most of us remember. I see no indication that nationalism is in decline. The number of nation-states is increasing, not decreasing.

MR. BERDAHL: Who wants to start? You can start with the question of public education. That may be the easier question.

MR. DE LA FUENTE: I have two brief comments, the first regarding secondary education. In Mexico—I'm not sure if this is true in other Latin American countries—some universities, like my own National Autonomous University of Mexico, oversee a significant portion of secondary education in Mexico. That has advantages and disadvantages.

An advantage is that we can set the standards for an important segment of public secondary education in Mexico. A disadvantage is that our faculty and administrative personnel spend much of their time ensuring that those standards are met and interacting with the secondary education faculty. So after a while, they lose their interest in collaborating.

For instance, we have groups that work constantly on committees that oversee secondary education for the sciences, reviewing their programs. That goes on for a while until the science faculty lose interest.

That also becomes a social problem, because you can no longer complain about the level of competence of the students that you're receiving because supposedly you have been overseeing their curriculum.

Regarding the decline of the nation-state and the increasing nationalism that you mentioned, I think both things are happening. We're seeing the decline of the nation-state because of the economic forces of globalization. This is happening in Europe, in other parts of the world, and to a lesser extent in America, with NAFTA. Nationalism has been aroused more as an emotion and as a subjective component of culture, and not necessarily with specific aims.

MR. BROERS: I'll make just a brief comment on the education factor. You put your finger on a very interesting topic, but I think there are two sides to this. In the United Kingdom we have a very good secondary education system. People express reservations about it, but the quality of the students we get is quite high, especially in the sciences. But that's because they have overspecialized. Some science students in the U.K. do nothing but physics and math from the age of fifteen. I disapprove of that, but it does mean that the students reach a relatively high level in those subjects.

School education in the United States, while not taking students as far in specialized subjects at a given age, is broader. As a result, you produce people who are better able to operate across a broader front and therefore may be more innovative.

We have been bemoaning the fact that the standard of math has been falling. I am prepared to tolerate that, provided it is replaced with some understanding, for example, of languages, or of the arts and humanities. But that's a very difficult balance. School education in the United States, while not taking students as far in specialized subjects at a given age, is broader. As a result, you produce people who are better able to operate across a broader front and therefore may be more innovative.

So I wouldn't be too harsh on the U.S. system—the grass is always greener on the other side of the fence. I would like our system to be broader—more like your system. The trouble is that students then need to stay in undergraduate education for five years. We have traditionally only kept them for three. We have just gone to four years for many science subjects, but this significantly increases costs.

JUDITH RODIN, President, University of Pennsylvania: Our colleague, Richard Atkinson, is leading a national discussion of standardized tests and their role in determining admissions to our universities

You represent a tradition, at least two of you, of very rigorous formal tests for admission. Other systems have a more open standard. I wonder whether you are experiencing pressure over the nature of that testing and the nature of the admissions process that uses it?

MR. BROERS: Yes, we are. We are looking intensely at SATs as a complement to the use of A-levels. We hear that many people in the States say that SATs are unreliable, but we feel A-levels are inadequate. I think Singapore has made a wise choice by deciding to use a combination of A-levels and SATs.

There's a rough correlation between A-levels and SATs. What we are anxious about is that some of the excellent private schools in England, such as Eton, have a much better record in achieving high A-level scores than do state schools. This introduces the possibility that students from underprivileged backgrounds may be disadvantaged. The thought is that the SAT is less sensitive to the standard of teaching and gives a truer measure of a student's underlying capability.

The data are unclear, however, and U.K. universities generally are against introduction of the SAT.

MR. BERDAHL: I want to thank the panel once again for a wonderful presentation. Thank you all.

5

THE IMPACT OF
INFORMATION TECHNOLOGIES
ON UNIVERSITIES

APRIL 23, 2001

During the first panel this morning, Sir Alec Broers demonstrated for us the empowering nature of information technologies when he was unable to get his slides on the screen. And Juan Ramón de la Fuente gave us a little insight into the psychiatric implications of waiting for audio-visual equipment to warm up. With that I will turn things over to Alan Gilbert to chair this second session on information technology.

Alan Gilbert is vice-chancellor of the University of Melbourne. After earning a doctoral degree in modern history from the University of Oxford in 1973, he taught history at universities in Australia and Papua, New Guinea, before becoming pro-vice-chancellor at the University of New South Wales in 1988 and subsequently vice-chancellor of the University of Tasmania in 1991. He became vice-chancellor of the University of Melbourne in 1996.

Published widely in British and Australian history, he was joint general editor of an eleven-volume history of Australia to celebrate the nation's bicentenary in 1988. He is a fellow of the Australian Academy of Social Sciences and chairman of Universitas 21, an international association of research-intensive universities.

—Charles M. Vest
President, Massachusetts
Institute of Technology

Introduction

Alan D. Gilbert
Vice Chancellor, University of Melbourne

O n behalf of the two oldest universities in Australia—Sydney and Melbourne, both kindly invited to this symposium—I, too, congratulate AAU on its centenary.

Is higher education in the midst of a global revolution? Universities are among history's most robust institutions. As we heard yesterday, it has not been through one defining "idea of a university" that they have worked their civilizing alchemy over more than 900 years; it is through many evolving ideas of what a university is and what it stands for.

For much of that history the very idea of a secular university would have been incomprehensible. Yet in cultures shaped by the Enlightenment, any appeal to faith-based knowledge now founders on the idea of a university as a place where rational inquiry and the remorseless logic of empirical falsifiability hold sway.

Similarly, while the idea of the research university has been extant for little more than a tenth of the long institutional history of the Western university, many of us in the modern academy now find it entirely normative.

Yet certain enduring characteristics of the university have retained their original significance across the centuries. One of them surely has been the idea of a university as a scholarly place where truth is pursued through reasoned and disciplined inquiry, and where knowledge is valued, preserved, transmitted, advanced, and applied. Another, just as surely, has been the idea of a university as a cultural bridge across the generations for what Matthew Arnold once called "the best that is known and thought in the world."

The third characteristic throughout nearly a millennium of flux has been the role of the university as a chartered or licensed monopoly for the assessment and certification of higher learning.

Until quite recently, a fourth enduring motive would have been the idea of a university as a physical place: a campus or network of campuses home to a face-to-face learning community.

Will such verities survive our lifetimes? In the presentations that follow you will hear that overused word "revolution." Is it being used for once without hyperbole? For whether we recognize it or like it or not, we may be caught up in a higher education revolution that is subverting, not the ever-evolving idea of a university, but certainly some of the enduring characteristics that have hitherto defined that idea.

Is that what our future portends? Will the 900-year monopoly that universities have enjoyed by virtue of their exclusive charters for the awarding of legitimate higher education degrees, diplomas, and cognate awards endure the burgeoning of new kinds of educational and training institutions?

> We may be caught up in a higher education revolution that is subverting, not the ever-evolving idea of a university, but certainly some of the enduring characteristics that have hitherto defined that idea.

The very word "university" has its origins in the Latin "universitas," used in medieval Europe to describe manufacturing or trading guilds that operated as privileged monopolies. We do well to remember that most of those ancient guild structures that flourished in preindustrial economies have long since been swept away as massive, sustained demand generated industrial revolutions in industry after industry over the last 225 years. This was, indeed, a key process in the making of the modern world.

We should remember that the old institutions always enjoyed an Indian summer of immense expansion as unprecedented demand began to build. They expanded their numbers and they increased their output. They tried valiantly to contain the new wine of heady technological innovation and demand growth within the ancient wineskins of monopolistic guild structures.

So it has been with the ancient idea of a university. The great boom of building universities and expanding campuses that has accompanied the rise of mass higher education in the world since 1945 is a pattern familiar to economic historians in other industries. Why should we expect the denouement to be different in the case of higher education? When demand pressures become inexorably strong, inherited monopolies are, in the end, challenged by new providers using new technologies and offering new modes of service.

You will have guessed rightly from those words that I am biased. I've spent much of the last year working on the idea of a new kind of university, a global online university that, when it is established in the next couple of months, will be called "U-21 Global." It will provide Universitas 21—an international network of research-led universities, or, if you like, a different kind of guild for a different kind of century—with a vehicle with which to contribute something to the solving of the problem that Henry Rosovsky diagnosed yesterday: how to bring higher education to 85 percent of the world where traditional solutions are demonstrably inadequate.

Like many that try to pick winning strategies in the midst of revolutionary change, I'm quite likely to be wrong in many respects. But these things I know to be true: there are 30 million people in the world today who are fully qualified to enter a university but for whom no university place is available. Within ten years, there will be 100 million of these university-ready people. Most of them will be in Asia, but many also will be in Latin America and Africa, with significant numbers in Europe and some even in the United States. Along with many "lifelong learners," also poorly provided with higher education and advanced training, they will be demanding access to advanced professional skills in an emerging global knowledge economy.

This also is true: there is simply no hope of this unmet demand being met by the traditional, expensive model of the campus-based university.

The old wineskin is stretching to the breaking point, but the new technologies and new models perhaps are at hand. In our lifetime, the idea of a university will be reinvented once again, this time at that great intersection between the virtual and the real that is the engine of change in our generation.

Campus-based universities will, of course, survive and thrive, but they will have no monopoly over the future. Where the virtual meets the real and the two are enriched at that conjunction, there higher education will, in our lifetimes, find its industrial revolution. That context, as well as the eminence of the presenters, makes this session profoundly important.

James J. Duderstadt is president emeritus and professor of science and engineering at the University of Michigan. He is well known to almost all of you. He was Michigan's president from 1988 to 1996.

Dr. Duderstadt's teaching and research interests range from nuclear fission reactors, thermonuclear fusion, high-powered lasers, and computer simulation, to science policy, higher education, and information technology.

He has received numerous national awards, including the National Medal of Technology for Exemplary Service to the Nation, and has been elected to many honorary societies and served on or chaired numerous public commissions and private boards.

—Charles M. Vest
President, Massachusetts
Institute of Technology

Prepare for the Revolution: The Impact of Information Technology on the Future of the Research University

James J. Duderstadt
President Emeritus, University of Michigan

I SHOULD FIRST NOTE WHAT A JOY IT IS TO BE BACK WITH THIS GROUP—EVEN more so for only an hour. The first lesson of information technology is never to trust it, particularly when you are going to give a lecture. A second lesson—unrelated to information technology—is never to trust the title that others attach to your talk. My title is, "Prepare for the Revolution." Now, having been a university president and recognizing the stresses on my colleagues, I realize that "revolution" is not a word that we use in this company, because it is liable to trigger a mass exodus of presidents toward the door.

The third understanding I've had for many years is that the protocol for a university president speaking before this group is best summarized by the phrase, "three points and a prayer." That is, you are allowed to make three

Digital technology will transform not only the activities of the university—teaching, research, outreach—but also how we're organized, financed, and managed, even whom we regard as our students and our faculties.

points, which is precisely what I am going to do, and then you pray as your colleagues tear you apart.

Let me begin by summarizing briefly my three points, and then I'll go back over them in some detail.

Point one is that the exponential evolution of digital technology is likely to continue for at least the foreseeable future. It will continue to drive rapid, profound, unpredictable, and frequently discontinuous change. It is a disruptive technology. It erodes—indeed, it obliterates—conventional constraints of space, time, of monopoly. It reshapes the boundaries of institutions.

Point two is that digital technology will transform not only the activities of the university—teaching, research, outreach—but also how we're organized, financed, and managed, even whom we regard as our students and our faculties. It could well lead to a restructuring of the current higher education enterprise into a global knowledge and learning industry.

Point three: As universities attempt to grapple with the challenges and opportunities presented by the digital age, they need to focus first on the fundamentals—on their values, their roles, their mission. They need to determine first what they need to strive to retain, and then how they must change to protect those characteristics.

My remarks today are shaped in part by my role for the past year as chair of a major study commissioned by the national academies in the United States (which include the National Academy of Sciences, the National Academy of Engineering, and the Institute of Medicine) to understand the implications of rapidly changing information technology for the future of the research university.

The steering group that has guided the project consists of many of your colleagues—Nils Hasselmo, Frank Rhodes, Joe Wyatt, Marye Ann Fox, Shirley Jackson, and Ralph Gomery—along with the chief technical officers of major technology companies such as IBM, Lucent, and Xerox, and experts in federal research and technology policy.

Let me begin by stating the obvious: it is a time of great

As universities attempt to grapple with the challenges and opportunities presented by the digital age, they need to focus first on the fundamentals—on their values, their roles, their mission.

change for higher education. The forces driving change are many and varied—the globalization of commerce and culture, the lifelong educational needs of citizens in a global economy driven by knowledge, the exponential growth of new knowledge and new disciplines, and the compressed time scales and nonlinear nature of the transfer of knowledge from campus laboratories into the commercial marketplace.

Of particular importance is the impact of information and communications technologies on the university. Modern digital technologies such as computers, telecommunications, and networks are reshaping both our society and our social institutions. They vastly increase our capacity to know and to do things, to communicate, and to collaborate. They allow us to transmit information quickly and widely, linking distant places and diverse areas and endeavors. They allow us to form and sustain communities for work, for play, and for learning in ways unimaginable a decade ago. They change the relationship between people and knowledge and, therefore, are likely to reshape in profound ways knowledge-based institutions such as universities.

> Technology is creating an open learning environment in which the student is evolving into an active learner and consumer of educational services, stimulating the growth of powerful market forces that could dramatically reshape the higher education enterprise.

Of course, this is nothing new to us. Higher education already has experienced significant change driven by digital technology. Our management and administrative processes depend heavily on it, as indicated by the millions of dollars we spent to reengineer our systems for the year 2000.

Research and scholarship also are highly dependent on information technology: computers simulate physical phenomena, networks link investigators, and digital libraries provide scholars with access to vast knowledge resources. Technology also will have a profound impact on teaching, freeing the classroom from the constraints of space and time and enriching learning by providing students with access to original source materials.

And yet, while this technology has the capacity to enhance and enrich teaching and scholarship, it also poses threats. We can now use powerful computers and networks to deliver educational services to anyone at any time in any place, no longer confined to the campus or the academic schedule. Technology is creating an open learning environment in which the student is evolving into an active learner and consumer of educational services, stimulating the growth of powerful market forces that could dramatically reshape the higher education enterprise.

Most believe the university will survive the digital age, but few deny that it could change dramatically in form and character. Knowledge is both a medium and a product of the university as a social institution. Hence it is reasonable to suspect that a technology that is expanding our ability to create, transfer, and apply knowledge by factors of 100 to 1,000 every decade will have a profound impact on both the mission and function of the university.

In the United States, the national academies have a unique mandate to monitor and sustain the health of the nation's research universities as key elements of the national research enterprise and the source of the next generation of scientists, engineers, and other knowledge professionals. This role becomes particularly important during periods of rapid change. It was from this perspective that last year the presidents of our national academies launched a project to understand better the implications of information technology for the future of the research university.

The premise of the effort was simple—that the rapid evolution of digital technology will present many challenges and opportunities to higher education in general, and to research universities in particular. But these issues are neither well recognized nor understood by university leaders and those who support and depend upon their activities.

The first phase of the project was aimed at addressing three sets of issues. First, to identify those technologies that were likely to evolve in the near term (a decade or less) and that could have a major impact on the research university. Second, to examine the possible implications of those technologies for the research university: its activities (teaching, research, service, outreach); its organization, structure, management, and financing; and its impact on the broader higher education enterprise and the environment in which it functions. And third, to determine what role, if any, our federal government and other stakeholders have in the development of policies, programs, and investments to protect the valuable role and contributions of the research university during this period of change.

Over the last year, the steering group met several times to consider these issues—including site visits to major technology centers such as Bell Laboratories and IBM Research Laboratories—and drew on the expertise of the National Academy complex.

This past January, we drew together 100 leaders from higher education, the technology industry, and the federal government to discuss these issues. That workshop is now being streamed through the Web servers of the Research Channel.

The insights of this very diverse group of participants revealed a certain consensus of views on the impact of the technology and its evolution. That consensus will form the basis for my discussion of the three points I mentioned at the outset. Let me return to them.

> Speculation about both the evolution and the impact of this technology has been notoriously incorrect. We generally overestimate the near-term but underestimate the long-term effects.

Point one. The extraordinary pace of change in information technology will not only continue for the foreseeable future, but could well accelerate on a super-exponential slope.

For the first several decades of the information age, the evolution of hardware technology followed the trajectory predicted by "Moore's Law"— a 1965 prediction by Intel founder Gordon Moore that the chip density and consequent computing power obtainable at a given price doubles every eighteen months. Although the law was intended to describe the evolution of silicon-based microprocessors, it turns out that almost every aspect of digital technology has doubled in power roughly every twelve to eighteen months, with some technologies, such as photonics and wireless technology, evolving even more rapidly.

Put another way, digital technology is characterized by an exponential pace of evolution in which characteristics such as computing speed, memory, and network transmission speeds for a given price increase by a factor of 100 to 1,000 every decade, decade after decade.

Of course, speculation about both the evolution and the impact of this technology has been notoriously incorrect. We generally overestimate the near-term but underestimate the long-term effects. With this caveat in mind, let me share with you a few data points.

This year a new generation of supercomputers is coming on line, so-called terascale computers capable of performing more than one trillion calculations per second. In laboratories right behind them is the next generation of machines running 100 times faster to address calculation-intensive applications such as protein folding.

New displays are now capable of producing resolutions that are considerably better than paper, at least to the eye. Retinal displays that use lasers to create images directly on the retina should give us, within the next decade or so, the possibility of 360-degree immersive environments.

Bandwidth is continuing to increase rapidly, with terabit-per-second network backbones and gigabit-per-second local area networks.

Even more significant is the explosion of wireless technologies, the so-called G3 or Internet-enabled technologies that are appearing throughout the world.

Applications software also is advancing rapidly, stimulated by new software paradigms such as genetic algorithms and new forms of collaboration such as open source development. Linux is the example.

If information technology continues to evolve at its present rate, by the year 2020 the thousand dollar notebook computer will have a data processing speed and memory capacity roughly comparable to the human brain.

Today the Internet links together hundreds of millions of people. Estimates are that within a few years this number will surge to billions—a significant fraction of the world's population. This growth will be driven in part by the fact that most economic activity will be based on digital communication.

By the end of next year, more than 90 percent of homes and 98 percent of schools in the United States will be linked to the Internet.

Bell Laboratories suggests that within the next two decades a "global communications skin" will evolve, linking together billions of computers that handle the routine tasks of our society, from driving our car to maintaining our health. Indeed, when we visited Bell Labs they pointed out that their current slogan is "fiber to the forehead." I'll let you imagine what that means.

Put another way, over the next decade we will evolve from giga-technology, denoting speed, storage, and data transmission rates in the billions; to tera-technology, in the trillions; and then to peta-technology, a million billion. To illustrate with a particularly extreme example, if information technology continues to evolve at its present rate, by the year 2020 the thousand dollar notebook computer will have a data processing speed and memory capacity roughly comparable to the human brain. However, it will be so tiny as to be almost invisible, and it will communicate with billions of other computers through wireless technology.

Digital technology provides unusual access to knowledge and knowledge services (such as education) hitherto restricted to the privileged few.

From the point of view of individuals planning the future of organizations, I think it is safe to assume that by the end of the decade we will have, at least compared to current technology, essentially infinite bandwidth and infinite processing power. We'll denominate the number of computer servers in the billions, digital sensors in the tens of billions, and software agents in the trillions. We'll evolve from "e-commerce," "e-government," and "e-learning" to "e-everything." Digital devices will increasingly become our primary interfaces not only with our environment, but also with people, groups, and social institutions.

Point two. The impact of information technology on the university likely will be profound, rapid, and discontinuous—just as it has been and will continue to be for corporations, governments, and other institutions.

At least for the near term, meaning a decade or less, we believe the research university will continue to exist in much its present form. However, meeting the challenge of emerging competitors in the marketplace will demand significant changes in how we teach, how we conduct scholarship, and how our institutions are financed.

Over the longer term, information and communications technology will drive very significant restructuring of our society and social institutions through what John Seely Brown and Paul Duguid of Xerox's Palo Alto Research Center have called the "6-D effects" of demassification, decentralization, denationalization, despecialization, disintermediation, and disaggregation. I would add to that a seventh D—democratization—because digital technology provides unusual access to knowledge and knowledge services (such as education) hitherto restricted to the privileged few.

How should research universities set priorities among their various roles—educating the young, preserving culture, critiquing society, conducting basic research and scholarship, and applying knowledge to serve society?

Just like the printing press, this technology not only enhances and broadly distributes access to knowledge, but in the process it shifts power away from institutions and to individuals.

Universities must anticipate these forces, develop appropriate strategies, and make adequate investments if they are to prosper during this period. Procrastination and inaction are the most dangerous courses for universities during a time of rapid technological change.

It is particularly important during a time of transformation to listen to the many stakeholders of the university—to learn of their changing needs, expectations, and perceptions of higher education, and to understand the forces driving change in our world.

Point three. It is our belief that universities should begin development of their strategies for technology-driven change with a firm understanding of those key values, missions, and roles that should be protected and preserved during the time of transformation.

Universities should begin by addressing the most fundamental questions. For example, how should research universities set priorities among their various roles—educating the young, preserving culture, critiquing society, conducting basic research and scholarship, and applying knowledge to serve society?

Which of its values and principles should be preserved, and which should be reconsidered—academic freedom, openness, critical thinking, commitment to excellence, shared governance, tenure?

How will research universities define their students? Are they young adults or established professionals? Are they the best and brightest, or members of the broader society, such as the workforce? Are they to be viewed at a local, national, or a global level?

How will we define our faculty members? As the products of our graduate schools and research laboratories, or as practicing professionals, in the manner of the University of Phoenix?

What is the role of the residential campus in a future in which knowledge-based activities such as learning become increasingly independent of space and time, perhaps even reality?

How should the research university address the rapidly evolving commercial marketplace for educational services and content? What policies need to be reconsidered? Intellectual property, copyright, instructional content ownership, faculty contracts?

What new financial models will be required? Beyond the need for making sustainable investments to acquire and maintain the technology, how can these models take into account the fact that the intensely competitive marketplace stimulated by digital technology could put at risk the current system of cross-subsidies in funding advanced education and research?

Just-in-time lifelong learning and the growing desire to be educated anywhere and at any time are driving demand for distance education. How should the research university approach the challenge and the opportunities of online distributed learning?

What is the role of our universities with respect to the digital divide—to the stratification of our society and our world with respect to access to technology?

Will more, indeed perhaps most, research universities find themselves collaborating and competing on a global scale? How will that square with the obligations of those institutions supported by local or regional governments?

Will new learning life forms—learning ecologies, if you will—evolve based on digital technology that could threaten the very existence of the university?

To prepare for an era of rapid change and uncertainty, institutions should realize that careful navigation toward distant goals may not be realistic. When traversing the whitewater rapids created by disruptive technologies, it may be challenging enough simply to keep the institution moving ahead without capsizing. Nevertheless, there are some steps that should be considered:

In this future of change universities should place a far greater emphasis on building linkages and alliances. These will allow individual institutions to focus on their unique strengths while relying on alliances to address the broader, diverse, and changing needs of society.

First, although learning and scholarship require some independence from society, it is particularly important during a time of transformation to listen to the many stakeholders of the university—to learn of their changing needs, expectations, and perceptions of higher education, and to understand the forces driving change in our world. This conversation provides the context for decision-making during a time of rapid technological change.

Second, since the future will become increasingly uncertain, universities should encourage experimentation with new paradigms for learning, research, and service. This means harvesting the best ideas from the academy and beyond, implementing the ideas on a scale sufficient to judge their effectiveness, and disseminating the results.

And, finally, in this future of change universities should place a far greater emphasis on building linkages and alliances. These will allow individual institutions to focus on their unique strengths while relying on alliances to address the broader, diverse, and changing needs of society.

Creative, visionary leaders can tap the energy created by new challenges to lead their institutions in new directions that will reinforce and enhance their most important roles and values.

The digital age poses many challenges and opportunities to the research university. The campus as a physical place, a community of learners, and a center of culture is likely to remain, at least for the near term. But the nature of its activities, its organization, its management, and its funding are likely to change quite rapidly and dramatically.

Emerging competition in the commercial sector could threaten our current financial models. We will be challenged to attract and retain outstanding students and faculty members in face of competition from institutions with superior technology environments, including the commercial sector.

Yet, while the challenge will be significant, so too will be the opportunities to enhance the important roles of the research university in our society. We suggest that university leaders should approach information technologies not as threats but as opportunities. Creative, visionary leaders can tap the energy created by new challenges to lead their institutions in new directions that will reinforce and enhance their most important roles and values. They can use digital technology to help their students learn more effectively, to help their faculty members become better teachers and scholars, and to enable their institutions to serve society better.

It is our collective challenge as scholars, educators, and academic leaders to develop a strategic framework that is capable of understanding and shaping the impact that this extraordinary technology will have on our institutions. We are on the threshold of a revolution that is making the world's accumulated information and knowledge accessible to individuals everywhere. Technology will link us together into new communities never before possible or even imaginable.

This has breathtaking implications for education, scholarship, learning, and, of course, for the research university in the digital age.

The respondent in today's session is Nannerl O. Keohane, president of Duke University since 1993 and previously president of Wellesley College. A distinguished graduate of Wellesley and Oxford, she completed her Ph.D. in political science at Yale University in 1967.

Dr. Keohane has talked and written extensively in the fields of political philosophy, feminism, and education. She was vice president of the American Political Science Association from 1988 to 1990.

Dr. Keohane serves on the boards of IBM, the Colonial Williamsburg Foundation, the National Humanities Center, and the Research Triangle Foundation of North Carolina. She is a fellow of the American Academy of Arts and Sciences and the American Philosophical Society, and a member of the Council on Foreign Relations. She has been awarded honorary doctoral degrees by numerous colleges and universities, including Dartmouth and Harvard, and was inducted into the Women's Hall of Fame in October 1995. She won the Golden Plate Award of the American Academy of Achievement in 1998.

—Alan D. Gilbert
Vice-Chancellor
University of Melbourne

"You Say You Want a Revolution?" Well …

Nannerl O. Keohane

PRESIDENT, DUKE UNIVERSITY

L**ET ME PUT MY OWN CARDS ON THE TABLE AT THE BEGINNING:** I SPEAK NOT as a latter-day Luddite, but as someone who finds information technology in higher education intriguing and powerful in many ways.

My own Duke University, like many others, has used distance education to good effect to bring together widely scattered audiences—MBA students on different continents, as well as nurses in rural hospitals in eastern North Carolina.

But my assignment is to put all this into some kind of historic perspective—and to remind us of features of the traditional university that we should try to preserve as we contemplate the coming revolution.

My tag-line quotation, in case you didn't recognize it, is from those forward-looking scholars, The Beatles. John Lennon's words, written in a highly revolutionary year, 1968, were as follows:

You say you want a revolution,
Well, you know,

We all want to change the world.
But when you talk about destruction,
Don't you know you can count me out.
Don't you know it's gonna be all right.
All right, all right.

In that vein, I will make four points, very concisely, so that we have ample time to discuss this fascinating topic.

First, the doomsayers are wrong. Second, predicting the future is very difficult. Third, quite a few things about the traditional university will endure because they are valued and valuable, whether or not we take any particular steps to preserve them. Fourth, some other features of our institutions are also very much worth preserving, but may well not be sustained unless we take special effort to protect them.

The Doomsayers are wrong

Everyone's favorite guru, Peter Drucker, made a prediction six or seven years ago. Thirty years from now, he said, the big university campuses will be relics. Already we are beginning to deliver more lectures and classes off campus via satellite or two-way video at a fraction of the cost. The college won't survive as a residential institution.

I am quite confident that he was wrong about that—superficial on one count and premature on the other. Drucker underestimated the cost of high-quality distance learning; as we have learned, these are very expensive things to do well, and we have not yet reaped any benefits from the technological revolution in terms of dramatic cost-cutting for an educational product of equal quality—although we will very probably find that we can do so in the future.

We have not yet reaped any benefits from the technological revolution in terms of dramatic cost-cutting for an educational product of equal quality.

And Drucker was far too pessimistic about the demise of universities. These are profoundly resilient institutions.

The advent of the printing press was regarded by some doomsayers as ending university education, since everyone could have easy access to information and would have little reason to undertake the arduous regime of the trivium or quadrivium. As we know, the academy changed in some ways but persisted, grew, and flourished in the new environment.

And I take some comfort from two predictions made about higher education more recently. One was an earlier version of Drucker forty or fifty years ago, in the form of several confident predictions that the invention of television would make schools and colleges obsolete. The other was an 1899 proposal from the commissioner of the U.S. Patent Office to the administration in Washington suggesting that the office be closed down on the grounds that everything had already been invented.

> Drucker was far too pessimistic about the demise of universities. These are profoundly resilient institutions.

Predicting the future is difficult and can even be dangerous
The new world of instructional technology is highly competitive, as institutions scramble to be the first to offer a particular kind of degree online or to develop new venues for our educational products. We assume, on shrewd historical evidence, that being first in the field and establishing a reputation as the obvious provider can bring considerable benefit.

But being on the "bleeding edge" carries peculiar risks, as well as formidable costs of start-ups and initial investments. The barriers to entry are substantial, and requirements include much more than the ability to design a great website.

In a book entitled *The Innovator's Dilemma*, Harvard Business School professor Clayton Christensen described how great companies have floundered when they ignored "disruptive technologies" that drove changes in economies, markets, and products. Such technologies are not immediately recognized as threats by mainstream institutions; at first, they seem eccentric or peripheral, so they are not taken seriously. In higher education, it is easy to argue that online learning is such a disruptive technology, and in many ways this undoubtedly is true.

However, one of the lessons of Christensen's book is that it is very difficult for mainstream leaders—all of us in this room—to know just what innovative technologies are going to do. If we could know that, we would never be blindsided.

I would argue that we are early enough in the infotech revolution that the same applies to us. It's clearly big, but big in what ways, and with what effects? To quote that great sage, Yogi Berra, "Never make predictions, especially about the future." Extrapolating from past trends is overly simplistic—

and overprediction about the "brave new world," as Prospero warned Miranda in *The Tempest*, is a risky affair. When the euphoria dissipates, the passionate belief in distance learning may encounter the same fate as passionate belief in the "new economy."

When the euphoria dissipates, the passionate belief in distance learning may encounter the same fate as passionate belief in the "new economy."

The message here, of course, is that—as with all revolutions—it is very difficult to predict the course that these new technologies will take, and foolhardy to assume that we can today see clearly the details of the path that lies ahead. Nonetheless, we have to be able to plan and navigate, not just drift, and formalizing strategy requires some predictions about the future. So I will do just that.

Durable traditional features of our institutions are likely to survive
While the revolution unfolds, there are some things that are likely to last, without requiring our special efforts to support or sustain them, simply because they are so valuable and valued.

One example is undergraduate residential education, developed in the United Kingdom and widely imitated around the world, especially in the United States.

This sort of education provides a distinctive combination of academic experience with other aspects of life we call "extracurricular"—social life, clubs of every conceivable variety, sports, dormitory living, volunteer service—all of which adds up to an eagerly awaited and nostalgically remembered part of life for many young people in our society.

The experience is valued for several reasons—some not particularly admirable, but no less durable for that—the reputational cachet of the degree, the proven financial benefits that come with it, and even the disinclination of parents to have eighteen-year-olds around the house for four more years earning their degrees online upstairs.

But some of the reasons we value the experience are more admirable. It can indeed be an important rite of passage, a way of developing and maturing that depends precisely on the context, the whole environment, the interplay of different activities in a very personal and direct experience. It is not possible to replicate that experience in cyberspace, and it is not likely to disappear in the near future.

A second example is the path to the Ph.D. Some research can be done online, of course, and many of the powers of new information technologies are enhancing doctoral education every day. But this is in no way a substitute for the mentoring that professors provide to doctoral candidates—a direct and personal experience that is very hard to replicate in all its fullness online.

These earliest and core scholarly experiences are thus likely to be sustained in something not too far from their traditional forms, I would predict. They will be enhanced and deepened by the powers of information technology, which bring as much to the curious first-year student as to the thesis writer. Information technology will allow for study abroad with connections to home, and for combinations of courses brought together in imaginative new forms. The possibilities are endless.

But the key factor here, and my major point this morning, is that it is precisely the combination of place and cyberspace that is so powerful, and this is almost certain to remain a dominant theme.

Cyberspace alone is a pale imitation of real physical contact, but cyberspace brings a whole new dimension to an education that also retains a spatial dimension. Places may change their character, but they will continue in some form to be crucial.

In every aspect of education—traditional, professional, executive, continuing—the ideal goal will be some distinctive combination, a combination different for each type of learning. In some—executive, continuing—cyberspace alone can be a pretty good substitute, even, in some cases, preferable. But the most interesting and durable forms of education, I would predict, will include both types of space.

> It is precisely the combination of place and cyberspace that is so powerful, and this is almost certain to remain a dominant theme.

As I'm sure most of us are aware, MIT recently made a breathtaking announcement: our colleagues there have decided to spend $100 million in the next few years putting instructional materials for all their courses on the web—lectures, syllabi, attachments, reading lists. The curious, bright high school student in Pakistan or the isolated scholar in Paraguay will be able to tap into the rich materials of MIT's great faculty immediately and at almost no cost beyond that of adequate communications equipment.

This indeed is a brave new world! Early reactions from some people were: "Won't this render an MIT education unnecessary?"

That seems very unlikely. Our colleagues are betting—and I agree—that it will simply enhance the sum of information available to others, provide models and examples, open new doors, increase knowledge powerfully for the whole world, and provide wonderful publicity and name recognition for MIT, making it even more likely that people around the world will want to come to Cambridge to learn even more from the authors of these syllabi or confer with them at their symposia.

The jury is still out on whether cyberspace connections, as fascinating and powerful and addictive as they apparently have become, create communities in any true sense.

In this connection, I would affirm with conviction, the durable appeal of intellectual community as the core of the university.

We keep hearing about the cyberspace "community" and how technology has enabled or will enable us to sustain virtual learning communities free from the tyranny of time and space. But the jury is still out on whether cyberspace connections, as fascinating and powerful and addictive as they apparently have become, create communities in any true sense—or whether the individual seated in front of her computer is still, in Robert Putnam's famous phrase, "bowling alone."

There will certainly be new types of institutions to provide new services, and familiar institutions will be changed and modified to perform new functions, but through all this universities will continue to do a pretty good job of organizing the way knowledge is delivered. The resilience that our institutions have shown in the past few decades will continue, I predict, to make these ancient institutions, in some recognizable form, durable and relevant in the years ahead.

Residential communities have challenged every generation of students to learn how to deal with difference—never more so than today. And never has it been more important to do so, given the increasingly close interconnections of our world.

There is also a third aspect of traditional universities that will survive: some loose, perhaps transforming version of our institutional core, our governance, structure, and support—what we call administration.

Networks will grow, yes, but anarchy is very unlikely to prevail—there will be structures for providing knowledge—and they will most likely be recognizable versions of universities.

We should not be too concerned about how closely these new structures will parallel our familiar forms. However, for the user—and, increasingly, for certain types of education, for the provider as well—online education can be considerably less expensive and far more convenient than place-based learning. This leads me to my fourth and final point.

Several more fragile features of our institutions are worth preserving
Some aspects of the traditional university may indeed become obsolete unless we make deliberate efforts to support them for the important values they bring.

Access, especially to undergraduate campus-based education, is one such feature. The danger is that as more and more varieties of online degrees become available, including baccalaureates in cyberspace, and as they become less and less expensive as new technologies and new modes of delivery of knowledge are perfected, the baccalaureate residential experience will once again become the province of the wealthy and privileged—as it was up through the nineteenth century.

If this happens, both our societies and our universities will be impoverished. Education does not work nearly as well among homogenous students; they will have a very distorted view of the world, be less well prepared to manage and partner with diverse workforces and colleagues; their prejudices will be reinforced and their horizons left narrow. And many deserving young people who could profit greatly from the distinctive residential education and contribute much to the education of their fellows will never know this opportunity.

> The danger is that as more and more varieties of online degrees become available, the baccalaureate residential experience will once again become the province of the wealthy and privileged.

The solution? Renewed commitment to need-based financial aid and making university, government, and social resources available to support this priority.

Another feature that may need special protection is the sense of community and belonging among the faculty. We may well find that we need to provide deliberate incentives to sustain that sense and prevent the faculty from becoming independent contractors—deprived of the networks of cross-

Both our society and the universities—and all of the individuals involved—stand to lose in the longer term if the faculty's sense of belonging together disappears for good.

disciplinary contacts that a real community provides, immured in their narrow disciplinary networks and responsive mainly to the financial opportunities of the best deal for going online.

The durable thread here is the long experience of the benefits of such community for all concerned, even if individuals sometimes see their interests elsewhere. But both our society and the universities—and all of the individuals involved—stand to lose in the longer term if the faculty's sense of belonging together disappears for good.

The solutions lie in finding ways to encourage retention of membership in the academic community through appropriate rewards for online exploration and development of new intellectual property on campus rather than forcing those activities outside—and being ready to spend real dollars to recruit and retain committed teacher-scholars as full-time tenured members of the university community with reasons to care about the place and help steward it, rather than succumbing to the temptation of hiring contract employees who have no loyalty to the institution and no reason to feel committed to sustaining it.

A final example of university features that may need special protection is the strong and admirable tradition of providing—through research, outreach, and civic participation—service to the community, nation and world, something that is very difficult to do through cyberspace.

Over time, especially in the United States, through the land-grant universities and the great public universities and community colleges, and more and more through private institutions as well, we have compiled an admirable record of making a difference in our cities, our neighborhoods, our regions—through volunteering, involvement, leadership, example. In a time when other bulwarks of community and pro bono service are under increasing pressure, if we wish to sustain the many benefits of livable communities where people care about their schools and other benefits, it would be foolish indeed to let the historic and crucial participation of faculty and students in these enterprises be gradually dissolved.

Conclusion

Powerful forces—intellectual and financial—are moving higher education in the direction of increasing reliance on information technology. We are in an age of exploration: the landscape is still largely uncharted. We would do well to consider carefully what seeds we plant in this brave new world, so we can concentrate on cultivating those most likely to bear fruit for our students.

To end on an optimistic note, I quote from the Durban seminar cosponsored by the American Council on Education and CHET in August 2000. The author is not noted but may well be in this room.

We have compiled an admirable record of making a difference in our cities, our neighborhoods, our regions—through volunteering, involvement, leadership, example.

> If [universities] are not flexible enough, they may become redundant.... But if they are too flexible, they may cease to be universities, at any rate in a recognizable form. If they abandon their commitment to liberal learning, to critical knowledge, to disinterested scholarship and science—in other words if they sacrifice their core, their fundamental values on the altar of novelty—universities may not be worth defending.... Of all the institutions created by human effort it is difficult to find one more benevolent, more creative, more emancipatory, more dynamic than the University. It is hard to believe that such an institution will not continue to be central to our aspirations, individual and collective.

DISCUSSION

KARI RAIVIO, Rector, University of Helsinki, Finland: In this mind-boggling description of technological development, we must not forget the parallel development that occurs in the human mind. No matter how much information we transmit, it is the human brain that, in the final analysis, must digest that information.

Moore's Law states that the capacity of central processing units doubles every year-and-a-half. The human equivalent is the cerebral cortex. That also has increased in capacity and volume in a process called evolution. It took almost 1.5 million years for the cortical volume to double. So there is a millionfold difference in the rate of evolution in the biological and technological spheres.

Another parallel that might be useful is the rate of transmission. In your networks, you transmit giga- and terabytes at almost the speed of light—300,000 kilometers per second. In the brain, the process goes at the nerve conduction velocity of about 10 meters per second. In many instances the rate-limiting factor in research and education—in either transmitting or receiving information—is not in the machinery, it is in the brain.

I suspect that many of the clashes that you see, many instances of alienation and marginalization, have to do with the inability of the human mind to adapt to the vastly more rapid rate of technological evolution.

MR. DUDERSTADT: I appreciate your comments, because the Finns are providing us with one of the most interesting examples of how a society evolves to embrace this technology.

It is clear that not only projecting the future evolution of this technology but also understanding its impact on individuals and institutions is a very difficult thing to do. To be sure, the brain is limited to some degree. Neuroscientists tell us that the bandwidth of the optical nerve is limited to about a megabit per second. On the other hand, we already see changes in the way that young people use this technology to think and learn.

My office is located in a gigantic multimedia center populated day and night by thousands of students with almost unlimited access to information technology. It is apparent that this "plug-and-play" generation is using these tools in ways quite different from those of us raised in the precomputer era. They think and learn through interaction and collaboration, in ways quite different than our faculties teach them.

More generally, it has become clear that although we have made great strides in recent years in understanding how the brain works, we still do not have a scientific basis for understanding learning and learning institutions, much less how technology affects them. Here I might note that the National Science Foundation will soon announce the formation of several national "Science and Learning Centers" with the mission of researching just these subjects.

BETSY HOFFMAN, President, University of Colorado: One of the things that we don't pay enough attention to with the information revolution is that, at least for now, it actually is increasing the demand for on-campus education. More and more students who were never touched by a college education are coming online and then wanting the on-campus experience.

We are faced with a 30 percent increase in applications this year and can identify no demographic base for the increase. I know that others of you are facing a similar experience.

MS. KEOHANE: That's a very good point and a good example of why it is so hard to make predictions. In some ways, the responses to the information revolution may turn out to be ones that are quite the opposite of what, on simplistic grounds, you might expect.

ROBERT M. BERDAHL, Chancellor, University of California, Berkeley: If electronic networks move much faster than neuronetworks, they move infinitely faster than faculty decisionmaking.

If electronic networks move much faster than neuronetworks, they move infinitely faster than faculty decisionmaking.

I'm very concerned about whether or not the structures of our institutions are capable of making decisions with regard to the technology in a time frame that will keep events from overtaking us. Do you have any observations about that particular factor?

MR. DUDERSTADT: I would agree with the concern. Indeed, it is one of the factors that stimulated the National Academy study. We intend to address it in the next phase by hosting a series of town hall meetings on several university campuses to understand how to stimulate better awareness and engagement at the faculty level.

It is interesting that if you get two or three faculty members together and chat with them about these issues, they are as enlightened and frequently as resilient and flexible as you can imagine. But if you put them into groups called "departments" or "colleges" or "faculty senates," they stop in their tracks.

I remember what one of our colleagues, Frank Rhodes, once said in a moment of frustration: "The university faculty is the last constituency on the face of the earth that still believes that the status quo is an option."

Faculty resistance will pose a very significant challenge to institutions. But I think the most important thing right now is to get the conversation going on our campuses, to build awareness of the challenges and opportunities presented by information technology. Without that, you will not have the forces you need to stimulate the change.

> If you get two or three faculty members together and chat with them about these issues, they are as enlightened and frequently as resilient and flexible as you can imagine. But if you put them into groups called "departments" or "colleges" or "faculty senates," they stop in their tracks.

MS. KEOHANE: Traditional faculty decisionmaking wasn't one of the things I listed about the traditional university that we need to preserve. But, more seriously, this is a good example of how we may need to reorganize ourselves to find structures that will allow people to build trust and to delegate to administrators or other representatives decisions that need to be made quickly. We can't allow the traditional patterns, for all their virtues in some settings, to stand in the way of making choices that have to be made rapidly.

DAVID B. FROHNMAYER, President, University of Oregon: One of the discontinuities to which you pointed, Jim (Duderstadt), may be that different disciplines react in different ways to the acceleration of these technologies. One can see that science, engineering, and medicine have responded much more rapidly than the disciplines of the arts, social sciences, and humanities. The variability of response has raised a number of the perplexities that other speakers have presented.

How do you deal with those discontinuities—the different rates in the absorption and use of technologies—in settings where the traditional academy is deeply devoted to the learning community to which Nan Keohane and others gave their eulogies?

MR. DUDERSTADT: Here again, the world is full of surprises. It is our sense that many of the most exciting applications of information and communications technology are occurring in the arts and humanities. An excellent example is provided by the efforts of the Mellon Foundation to build and make available to scholars vast digital libraries of scholarly literature (the JSTOR project) and visual images (the ARTSTOR project).

Here I might note, as a former dean of engineering, my concerns that sometimes those of us most closely associated with the development of technology, scientists and engineers, are not nearly as innovative in its application as our colleagues in the arts and letters.

Universities should bear in mind this pervasive and unpredictable impact when determining how they invest in digital technology infrastructure.

> Sometimes those of us most closely associated with the development of technology, scientists and engineers, are not nearly as innovative in its application as our colleagues in the arts and letters.

LARRY R. FAULKNER, President, University of Texas at Austin: I'd like to comment on what Bob Berdahl just said about faculty decisionmaking. It is, of course, notoriously slow in its formal channels, but it is adaptive in informal channels. The adaptation of the university to the research agenda and the disciplinary evolution that has occurred in the postwar era have largely occurred through informal channels.

The pattern of evolution in universities is much less for formal faculty organizations to sit down, work out an agenda, and execute it than it is for informal clusters of faculty to set up programs and then present the governing organization with a *fait accompli*. That was true long before the stresses of information technology arrived, and I expect that those channels will continue to work.

L. DENNIS SMITH, President, University of Nebraska: What is the likelihood that groups of faculty, even from multiple universities, might come together and create shadow institutions in which they market their own courses, essentially independent of any of us?

MR. DUDERSTADT: There is certainly precedent for this type of behavior in the transfer of intellectual products from campus-based research. These spin-offs have created numerous—and hopefully very generous—millionaires among our faculties. Since there still is considerable uncertainty about whether intellectual property from instructional activities will take a similar path, we need to watch carefully interesting experiments such as MIT's "open course" learningware program, which aims to make much of the content of the university's curriculum publicly accessible. If MIT (and society) benefits more from this "public good" approach than from commercial development, it may establish a paradigm different from that used for the results of campus-based research.

MS. KEOHANE: I would give a slightly different answer. This may be an instance of what Alan Gilbert was talking about earlier in terms of a new guild—that there may be some guild-like behavior here. I would argue that these folks would be following in the path of their medieval forebears and reinventing the university. Eventually they would find that they need all the boring things that we in administration have labored so hard to provide. Once faculty members see their out-ahead colleagues trying to recreate that structure they will say, "Wow, they spent a lot of time and money, and we've got all of that right here." That's why I think that some people will take that path, but it will not become dominant.

MR. DUDERSTADT: We might even need university presidents, God forbid.

CHARLES E. YOUNG, President, University of Florida: I'd like to comment on what this revolution will end up producing. I've participated in the assimilation of the revolution of the 1960s and 1970s and the revolution of the open university. It seems to me that what we're really talking about is the university as a great assimilator. There is a revolution, but the university has shown that it is capable of assimilating changes of this kind and, in many respects, continuing to look very much like it did before.

Having left one university at which I spent a large part of my life and come to another, I've had the opportunity to test the views I had before. What has been said several times today is certainly true: the demand for what universities provide is growing apace with the changes in the way education can be delivered.

MR. DUDERSTADT: I would like to agree with you about the capacity of the university to assimilate revolutions and evolve over time. Yet as a scientist and engineer, I feel obliged to point out one significant difference with information and communications technologies. Most technologies, such as transportation and energy, follow an S-shaped curve over time, first evolving very rapidly and then leveling off as they reach a point of diminishing returns. However, information technology has evolved exponentially for nearly a century, with the power available for a given price increasing a hundredfold or a thousandfold every decade. There is every indication that this will continue for at least another two decades or more. This rapid evolution, coupled with its pervasive nature, makes information technology a "disruptive" technology, one with highly unpredictable consequences.

> As we look at a millionfold or billionfold increase in the power of digital technology, we may not even be able to understand the changes that will occur, at least within our present context.

Although we probably will not be able to predict its impact on the university in the near term (a decade or less), at least we will be able to understand technology-driven change when it occurs. Over the longer term, however, as we look at a millionfold or billionfold increase in the power of digital technology, we may not even be able to understand the changes that will occur, at least within our present context. It is this unique exponential evolution of the technology that raises concern about the future of the university in the digital age.

MARK WRIGHTON, Chancellor, Washington University in St. Louis: I'm a fan of technology, especially when it works. The advance of technology in this arena has been excellent, in many respects faster than many would have predicted. But there are a few extremely important areas where the advances have not kept pace.

One is the human-machine interface, which I think has been relatively slow to come along. It is increasingly the case that individuals are spending far more time sorting through the information that is coming their way. Could you comment on these problems?

MR. DUDERSTADT: I would agree with you. Although we increasingly view new information technologies as being as ubiquitous as the telephone, the occasional glitches suggest that there is still much about the human-machine interface that we do not understand. This is an area that deserves considerably more attention than it is currently receiving.

MS. KEOHANE: I would turn the tables and put on my IBM hat. Despite all the evidence that this is proving more difficult than we would have liked, the kinks will get worked out. Things will get better, and the human-machine interface will be less of a drag.

I don't know when. I can't give you a date. But I am less worried about that than I am about some of the unintended consequences. We'll keep getting it better; and I hope that it will be sooner rather than later.

MR. GILBERT: May I make one observation as a non-American? This has been very much an American discussion from the speakers and in the questions and comments. In conclusion, I ask you to remember what Henry Rosovsky said yesterday about the growing gap between the kind of community that is having this discussion now and the other 85 percent of the world. If that 85 percent is to produce the knowledge workers of Robert Reich's knowledge economy, one of the things that seems true to me as a non-American is that they simply will not be able to do it through the campus-based university model. It is simply too expensive. And they are too far behind now.

This revolution may be differential in its impacts and realities in different parts of the world. American society may have a very idiosyncratic educational experience.

I'd like to ask you to join me in thanking the speakers and, in thanking them, to thank yourselves for the quality of the discussion.

6

TRENDS IN INTERNATIONAL UNIVERSITY COLLABORATION

APRIL 23, 2001

Malcolm Gillis is the Ervin Kenneth Zingler Professor of Economics at and president of Rice University. He spent the first twenty-five years of his professional life teaching economics and bringing economic analysis to bear on important issues of public policy in nearly twenty countries, from the United States and Canada to Ecuador, Colombia, Ghana, and Indonesia.

The last decade of his career has been devoted primarily to university leadership, first at Duke University and then at Rice, where he was named president in 1993. His research and teaching have focused on two broad classes of issues and their national and international dimensions: fiscal reform and environmental policy.

—Charles M. Vest
President, Massachusetts
Institute of Technology

INTRODUCTION

Malcolm Gillis
PRESIDENT, RICE UNIVERSITY

I WOULD LIKE TO EXTEND A SPECIAL WELCOME TO THE PRESIDENTS, chancellors, and vice-chancellors from across the world. I was looking around the room this morning and counting the number of presidents and chancellors here from overseas universities. I've been privileged to visit just about half of them over the past four decades. I hope to have four more decades to visit the rest on their home grounds.

The history of the universities of AAU is rich with experience in international education. Some of the programs are longstanding and successful, like the Midwest Universities Consortium for International Activities, which the "Big Ten" Midwest schools established thirty-six years ago. A few others have foundered and disappeared. Now we are seeing renewed interest among AAU universities in a wide array of international ventures. Some of the new programs are quite ambitious; others have more limited objectives.

We are seeing renewed interest among AAU universities in a wide array of international ventures. Some of the new programs are quite ambitious; others have more limited objectives.

The University of Pennsylvania has new technology-based programs with India and Singapore. MIT has a two-year-old undertaking in distance education with Singapore, reinforced by faculty visits to the city-state. Duke University's international program at the Fuqua School of Business and the Duke program in Frankfurt are both heavily tied to distance learning and management. They have attracted worldwide attention.

At my own university, we are modestly involved in the beginning of a new private research university in Germany, the International University Bremen, or IUB, which is modeled along the lines of Rice University.

Among the more ambitious undertakings is the Association of Pacific Rim Universities, or APRU, founded in 1997. AAU provided an important model for APRU. Four of our members, led by the University of Southern California, co-hosted the inaugural meeting, and the eleven AAU universities on the West Coast are APRU's U.S. members.

APRU enhances mutual understanding among chief executives of member schools and facilitates cooperation in teaching and research among its thirty-four members in East Asia, Latin America, Canada, and the United States.

The organization already is officially recognized by the Asia Pacific Economic Cooperation group. That group expects APRU to help shape Pacific Rim policies on education, science, technology, and human resource development. It is truly an ambitious undertaking.

But Europe also is in the midst of a flowering of new higher education initiatives that reach across national borders. These undertakings are aimed at reforming higher education systems in ways that will lead to convergence and greater comparability. First came the Sorbonne Declaration in 1998, followed by the Bologna Declaration of 1999, involving twenty-nine nations in Europe.

The Bologna Declaration creates a well-defined European space for higher education. Far more than a political statement, it is a call for actions—not action, but actions—and should be very closely followed by all of us on this side of the Atlantic.

> Europe is in the midst of a flowering of new higher education initiatives that reach across national borders. These undertakings are aimed at reforming higher education systems in ways that will lead to convergence and greater comparability.

Ministers of higher education of the twenty-nine-member Bologna group will meet again in May. The architects of the Bologna Declaration are in close contact with the seventeen-member Association of Universities of Asia and the Pacific, which you heard about this morning.

Peter Gaehtgens is president of Free University of Berlin and a well-known physiologist. After earning a medical degree from the University of Cologne in 1964, he went on to become a university lecturer, assistant professor, and professor at that university. In 1967–69, he was a research fellow at the California Institute of Technology. In 1983, he was Forney Professor at the Institute of Physiology at Free University of Berlin. He became the institute's director in 1987.

He went on to serve as vice-president of the medical departments of the university, and then as dean of the Department of Human Medicine. In 1997, he became vice-president and acting deputy to the president. Two years later, in 1999, he became president. He is a full member of the Berlin-Brandenburg Academy of Sciences.

—*Charles M. Vest*
President, Massachusetts
Institute of Technology

University Collaborations Within Regions: The European Union Experience

Peter Gaehtgens
PRESIDENT, FREE UNIVERSITY OF BERLIN

W E PROBABLY ALL AGREE THAT INTERNATIONAL COLLABORATION HAS become an important element in university development world-wide. But why international cooperation is so important for any one university is less apparent. Scientific research, one of the central functions of universities, has always been international and cannot occur without international cooperation. This is not a new phenomenon. Why then is international cooperation between universities needed more today than ever?

This morning we heard an interesting alternative explanation of the phenomenon of international university cooperation presented by Shigehiko Hasumi from Tokyo University. According to his view, the emerging third generation of universities will differ from the second in structure, aims, and goals. Nation-states are disappearing, and globalization of the economy and labor markets is paving the way for the globalization of education. Indeed, the development of information technology, the increased mobility of people, and the migration of populations driven by economic, social, and political gradients will provoke cultural contact and the internationalization of public life, educational principles, and structures.

There are those who believe that in this context, the universities' main motive in seeking international collaboration is competition. The scientific productivity of a university depends most heavily on the creative individual researcher. Therefore, the recruitment of the best students and academic staff must be one of the central elements of university policy. However, outstanding academic staff have become more internationally mobile, and student recruitment no longer occurs from the protected national territory in which a given university has a monopoly. At the same time, a competitive worldwide market of science-based higher education and professional training has developed. Because great research universities increasingly operate and face competition everywhere, worldwide competition induces them to seek international collaboration in various forms.

Harmonizing different educational systems will always meet considerable obstacles because the principles laid down in an educational system represent the cultural identity of a nation.

In Europe, the general trend of closer cooperation between universities is paralleled and significantly reinforced by the process of building the political European Union. That process requires the development of close collaboration among many national educational systems, not only single universities. Since the collapse of the Soviet Union about a decade ago, the added task of reconciling educational systems of Eastern Europe has not made the process any easier.

Harmonizing different educational systems will always meet considerable obstacles because the principles laid down in an educational system represent the cultural identity of a nation. Traditions of thinking and feeling, language barriers, and cultural traditions must be recognized. In Europe, national passports have been given up, national borders have ceased to exist, and a common currency will be introduced on January 1, 2002. It may seem inevitable, therefore, that principles of university education throughout Europe will not remain dominated by individual national policies.

On the other hand, Europe as a region would lose much of her attractiveness to students and faculty from all parts of the world if, for instance, Italian universities could not remain Italian universities. So European universities face the challenge of developing global competitiveness while enhancing regional cooperation.

Much has already happened in Europe in response to that challenge. Various types of university collaborations, networks, and alliances have been developed, either with government encouragement and support or through individual university decisions. These collaborations are aimed at specific research activities and teaching programs, but, above all, they are tailored to enhance international exchange of students and academic personnel.

In principle, there is nothing new in Europe with respect to cooperation in scientific research. Collaborations between individual researchers are still the fundamental mechanism for developing projects and advancing young academics. With advanced communications technologies, such activities are not concentrated within a specific region. But they do require support for personal contacts such as international travel and visits to laboratories. Unfortunately, those needs are often forgotten in public discussions.

Research collaboration with institutional impact generally requires the identification of existing institutional strengths, as well as mechanisms for the participants to develop complementary and concerted actions. Research networks also require national or even supernational funding programs that specifically encourage interuniversity collaborations.

Top-down programs of collaboration have existed in the European Union for quite some time, but not all member countries are expert in using them. The British seem to do very well, but German universities are not as well organized as a group to overcome the substantial amount of red tape from Brussels. The result is that we pay in more than we receive.

In any event, top-down programs are of relatively minor importance compared to other research collaborations generated from the bottom up, as we shall see.

> The differences between national education systems create a substantial impediment to student mobility: credits and exams taken abroad often are not considered equivalent.

Since European countries organize their educational systems so differently, international collaboration can be very complicated. Indeed, the differences between national education systems create a substantial impediment to student mobility: credits and exams taken abroad often are not considered equivalent. Not even the structure of the academic year is the same all over

Europe: universities in some countries have academic years, while others have semesters and even trimesters.

As a result of this variability, a student transferring from one European university to another generally has to accept a loss of time. For that reason, it has been the policy of the EU to try to reduce the differences between educational systems within Europe.

In addition, both the European Commission in Brussels and various national governments have programs to encourage university collaboration within the Union. Although these programs require a significant contribution from participating universities, many European universities consider collaboration an important strategic goal.

The European job market has created strong pressures to increase student exchanges. Students with university experience abroad often are given preference by future employers.

Complementing these efforts, the European job market has created strong pressures to increase student exchanges. Students with university experience abroad often are given preference by future employers, not only because of better professional training or language proficiency, but because of their experience in different cultural settings.

The program of student and staff mobility called "Erasmus/Socrates" is one of the oldest, most expensive, and, some say, most effective programs initiated and financed by the EU to support collaboration among member universities. Since the 1980s the program has supported the exchange of students and academic staff, joint degree programs, development of curricula, international partnerships, and thematic networks.

To participate in student mobility, universities sign bi- or multilateral contracts that include the EU as a participating institution. Tuition fees are waived by the host university, which also provides special advisory services. Participating universities must recognize credits earned by their students abroad. (Many European universities charge tuition, while others, such as those in my own country, do not. Discussions are taking place all over Europe about whether universities that are not charging tuition should do so in the future, particularly in the face of reduced budget allocations from their governments.)

Student participants in the Erasmus/Socrates program sign a contract setting forth the courses to be taken during the time abroad. Erasmus/

Socrates does not cover the complete cost of study abroad, but it does cover travel expenses and the difference in average living costs. Remaining living costs must still be financed by the individual student—a significant impediment to expanding the program.

Recognizing the increasing importance of this form of university collaboration, some universities help support their exchange students by contributing to their living expenses. At my university, we believe that money for study abroad is well spent and solicit private funds for such purposes.

Over the past decade the number of students participating in EU mobility programs has reached about 100,000 per year. The numbers are still rising, especially since universities in Central and Eastern Europe began participating. Nearly 2,000 universities from EU-member states and associated countries, mostly in eastern Europe, have joined the Erasmus/Socrates program.

My university has contracts with 252 partner universities within the Erasmus/Socrates network. This year, we have nearly 1,000 exchange students: 576 incoming and 383 outgoing. The asymmetry results from the fact that some places in Europe are more attractive than others—this, too, is a problem for the program.

Support from the Erasmus/Socrates program contributes significantly to the 5,500 international students who attend my institution. International students represent about 12 percent of our student body, well above Germany's national average of 9 percent.

> Over the past decade the number of students participating in EU mobility programs has reached about 100,000 per year.

If European university collaboration and student education are to be significantly increased, certain difficulties must be eliminated. Academic credit is one.

The European credit transfer system (ECTS) was established as an instrument for translating and transferring course work and course assessment. As a common educational currency, ECTS is helpful in creating at least a minimum of curricular transparency.

In signing the Declaration of Bologna in 1999, the ministers of education of all EU member states declared their intention to attain the following objectives by the year 2010:

- Adoption of a system of easily readable and comparable degrees.
- Adoption of a system based on two main cycles: bachelor's and master's. The first cycle will last at least three years and provide an appropriate level of qualification for the European labor market; the second should lead to a master's or doctoral degree.
- Promotion of mobility by overcoming obstacles to free movment.
- Promotion of European cooperation in quality assurance.
- Promotion of necessary European dimensions in higher education.

Although we unanimously regard international collaboration for student mobility as important, some universities consider the Bologna Declaration too far-reaching. Countries such as Germany would be forced to completely change their national educational system to comply with European harmonization. There is great controversy about the replacement of the traditional one-cycle system of diploma and magister with the new concept of bachelor's and master's degrees. The defenders of tradition emphasize the potential loss of qualities like the Humboldtian unity of education and research.

The current situation is far from uniform. Some universities are changing from the traditional to the new system, while others have introduced a few specialty curricula using the new principles. Others simply refuse to adopt the new rule, arguing that students graduating with the new degree may face poor job prospects in the local market.

Eventually, though, given the strong political pressure and the long-term interests of the universities, university curricula within Europe will be completely harmonized.

Many universities have already established new curricula that follow the two-cycle system. These include several European master's degree programs. My university, for example, offers six such programs, including a master's degree in transatlantic studies that was developed in cooperation with six European and two U.S. universities. We also offer a joint master's degree program in political science with the Institut d'Études Politiques in Paris.

Also controversial is the discussion about supranational rules for accreditation and quality control. While systems of quality control are currently run by state and national governments, a nongovernmental, supranational replacement system is in the process of being implemented—or at least developed.

To coordinate collaborations among heterogeneous European universities, the Association of European Universities was established in March 2001 by a merger of the previous confederations of European rectors' conferences. The association now represents the presidents and rectors of more than 550 European universities. Its aims are to:

- Promote and safeguard university values and university autonomy
- Develop a coherent system of European higher education and research
- Support and guide members in their development and in enhancing their contributions to society
- Provide information and support the exchange of information and best practices among members
- Lobby at the national and European levels, especially before the European Union
- Encourage cooperation and networking among members
- Develop research and education partnerships between Europe and other regions of the world.

With the large number of participating universities, the most significant tasks of the association have been representing universities to the European political administration in Brussels and organizing the exchange of information.

Although large and influential associations are important and necessary, I consider a university's participation in small, international networks more effective— even if network programs often appear unfocused and their effectiveness limited to sharing information about European funding programs.

One of these smaller university networks, the Institutional Network of the Universities from the Capitals of Europe, or UNICA, receives special attention within Europe because of the special character of the cities in which its members are located. Founded in 1990, UNICA has the following goals:

- To strengthen and structure collaborations between universities in higher education, research, training, and high administration
- To promote common strategies and projects
- To centralize and circulate essential information about European programs, cooperative agreements, and more
- To facilitate and promote contacts and exchanges of information and experience.

UNICA's twenty-nine-member universities are located in twenty-five European capitals. Members profit both from their specific political and social environments and from their close-range interaction with their national governments. One of the outstanding activities of UNICA has been the European Students Conference, initiated and organized by the Freie Universität Berlin under the joint patronage of French president Jacques Chirac and German chancellor Gerhard Schroeder. Last November, 240 student delegates from twenty-six universities in twenty-three European countries came together to share their vision of European policy in the twenty-first century. The results were published in the form of a memorandum. A follow-up conference is planned at University College London in 2002.

Our universities are not limiting collaboration to fellow institutions in Europe but are seeking also to network with selected American, Asian, African, and Australian universities of similar size and purpose.

My university currently enjoys ninety-two international partnerships in all parts of the world. About one-third of AAU's members are affiliated with Freie Universität Berlin, as are about one-third of the other international universities represented at this meeting. We benefit greatly from these direct bilateral partnerships in terms of student and staff exchanges and cooperation. Indeed, the problems frequently associated with international student exchange, such as tuition, can be alleviated through agreements between partners.

The problems frequently associated with international student exchange, such as tuition, can be alleviated through agreements between partners.

Yet even more promising is the development of small, nonexclusive strategic alliances of international universities that share similarities in structure, goals, and potential. Because the universities in such alliances are carefully selected, they are better able to develop well-integrated programs of teaching and research, provide intensified and continuous exchange of teaching personnel, share in extracurricular activities such as alumni work, and even recruit international faculty.

International faculty recruitment is particularly important. Unless our universities recruit faculty members from around the world, they will not become truly international universities that attract students from the entire world. Although my university is working hard to recruit international faculty members, that task would be much easier with the support of a small university alliance that helped us raise our international profile.

We are discussing the potential of such intensified international interaction in a strategic alliance with New York University, Universiteit van Amsterdam, and University College London—four of the world's great metropolitan, research-led universities. As one step toward providing an integrated response to globalization, we are developing joint master's programs that will build on complementary strengths, different cultural and educational traditions and approaches, and different political, geographical and social conditions to provide an educational experience not obtainable in a single country.

There are a large number and a wide spectrum of university collaborations in Europe: individual cooperation between university members, small alliances, larger networks, and national and supranational programs. The large institutionalized networks deal with the very complex harmonization of higher education and research within the EU, and they deeply influence the political environment in which a single university in Europe can act. The development of European universities thus is—and will continue to be—tightly connected with the development of the political union in Europe.

Many European universities, however, continue to look for partners around the globe. But internationalization is a difficult task, particularly for universities in countries where the English language does not come with mother's milk. Partners in university collaboration must be chosen carefully. While I consider EU programs like Erasmus/Socrates of utmost importance in supporting and improving student mobility, in the future, the emphasis for individual universities will be on small alliances of selected partners with comparable academic structure, status, research profile, and standing.

Thank you very much.

M. Peter McPherson is president of Michigan State University. He has had wide and fruitful experience in government in the United States and in the private sector. In government, he was at the White House, the U.S. Treasury Department, the U.S. Agency for International Development, the Overseas Private Investment Corporation, and, very early in his career, the Internal Revenue Service.

He was a youthful assistant to President Gerald Ford, and from 1981 to 1987 was chair of the board of the aforesaid Overseas Private Investment Corporation. He also served as administrator of the U.S. Agency for International Development from 1981 to 1987. After serving another two years as deputy secretary of the treasury, he joined Bank of America, where he focused on global debt restructuring and managed the bank's work in Latin America and Canada.

He became president of Michigan State University in 1993. He has received the U.S. secretary of state's Distinguished Leadership Award, the U.S. Presidential Certificate of Outstanding Leadership, and the UNICEF Award for Outstanding Contributions to Child Survival.

University Collaborations Across Regions: Problem Solving and Institution Building

M. Peter McPherson
President, Michigan State University

I WOULD LIKE TO TALK THIS AFTERNOON ABOUT THE GROWING KNOWLEDGE gap between poor countries and the rest of the world, a gap that saps the strength of universities in poor countries and reduces their ability to educate students, solve national problems, and stimulate economies. Although the gap affects poor countries the most, middle-income countries are not immune from its effects.

It is interesting to look back over the generations, both in developed and developing countries, and realize that universities have been very independent entities. Our faculties have cooperated in the past and even more in recent times. But as institutions, we have not worked together nearly as deeply or as closely as we might have done, despite some well-funded exceptions in the big sciences.

From Michigan, I look south to Indiana, where Indiana University and Purdue University established a joint campus in Indianapolis. That close institutional collaboration was an exception in this country and, I think, around the world.

Consider the contrast between the independent behavior of our educational institutions and the collaborative behavior of the private sector. For decades now, joint ventures and mergers have become steadily more common—a phenomenon not found in the university community. It is fair to ask—not whether the phenomenon is good or bad—but why it has occurred in one sector and not the other.

For decades now, joint ventures and mergers have become steadily more common—a phenomenon not found in the university community.

Several factors account for the difference. Fundamentally, universities have not seen compelling reasons, either economic or mission-related, to collaborate. I'm not saying the reasons have never existed, only that I don't think the case for cooperation has been as compelling as in the business world. We haven't had to publish quarterly profit-and-loss statements. We haven't had a market to press us.

Another factor is our decentralized decision-making structure, which leads us to make incremental changes.

By almost any measure, our reluctance to collaborate is beginning to change. Clearly it is changing in developed countries, as we have heard today. Consider the United States. What a major step it was to create Internet2! Internet2 started with thirty-two universities; it now numbers about 180. But the change also shows in our work with developing countries.

Why are we now seeing compelling reasons for cooperation that were not present a generation ago? For one thing, issues today are more global. Mad cow disease affects more than a single country, and the movement of diseases from animals to humans is a major concern. There's just no way you can leave out part of the world when dealing with issues of health, environment, and security. The list of such issues is long.

This morning, our colleague from Mexico made a compelling case about the integration of Mexico, Canada, and the United States. But with our close-knit, integrated, almost global economy, the case goes beyond regionalism. With our companies becoming global entities, educational institutions, too, are being pressed to go global—in outlook and action.

Shigehiko Hasumi from the University of Tokyo made an excellent point about his country that applies to the rest of us as well: As nation-states begin to change their character, people are less likely to think only of their own country. That's why we are seeing more true integration and collaboration.

Look at some of the things that are happening in developing countries. Four major U.S. foundations recently decided to build four universities in Africa. With World Bank president James Wolfensohn advocating more work in higher education, the Bank will be investing more in technology so that interuniversity linkages can be closer and deeper.

Cornell announced a few days ago that it was spending $750 million to create a branch of its medical school in Qatar. Whether or not residents of Qatar call themselves a developing country, that certainly is a huge international involvement by any measure.

Behind much of the change lies technology: the ease, the convenience, and the economies that it offers.

MIT stunned the world a few days ago by announcing that it would provide courseware and curricular materials on the Web—in effect, providing textbooks for the world. I wouldn't be surprised if other universities join in. This is an exceedingly important and historic step.

Around the world universities are connecting more and more. If students can be anywhere, so, too, can professors. At Michigan State, a Jewish studies course will be taught jointly next year by a professor in Israel and a professor on our campus. We are going to see a lot more of this kind of collaboration.

The same trend is apparent in research. One of the areas I know well is agricultural research. For some time, the Agency for International Development has been funding Collaborative Research Support Programs focused on particular crops important in poor countries. Seven or eight U.S. universities with research strengths in these crop areas are working together and beginning to broaden their collaborations.

> MIT stunned the world a few days ago by announcing that it would provide courseware and curricular materials on the Web—in effect, providing textbooks for the world.

Why shouldn't universities from the affected developing countries also participate? Donors already are saying they want that kind of collaboration because, in fact, that's the best way to solve problems.

Last night, the Aga Khan mentioned the digital library. Many questions remain on how to achieve such a library, notably questions of copyright. It is a complicated problem. But for the same reasons that drug companies decided to cut the cost of drugs for AIDS victims in developing countries, we need to offer textbooks on the Web. We need to make these materials available for the same compelling reasons of international development.

Let me stir things up a bit. If we're really going to reduce the knowledge gap, we also must make scholarly publications available to developing countries on the Web.

In 1995, according to UNESCO, nearly 39 percent of scholarly publications came from the United States, about 35 percent from Western Europe, and 10 percent from Japan and the newly industrialized Asian countries. In short, some five-sixths of the total came from the group that presumably has the capacity to pay for them—though, like all of you, I wonder about that some days.

Libraries in the United States pay some $2.5 billion a year now for those publications. You all know how it works. The U.S. government gives our faculty research grants. A major piece of those grants is spent on publications. The universities pay some portion—maybe a lot—of the salaries of those faculty. Then, when the faculty member writes the article and gets it published, he or she must, in effect, give away the copyright to the publisher. Then we all buy the published articles back at prices that are substantially higher than inflation increases. It is a truly vicious cycle.

If we're really going to reduce the knowledge gap, we also must make scholarly publications available to developing countries on the Web.

On my campus, library budgets are increasing substantially faster than budgets for the campus as a whole. I suspect that's true for virtually every one of you here in the United States, and no doubt abroad, as well.

If we have trouble with this here in the United States, think of the situation of countries such as those that emerged from the former Soviet Union. So much of the world simply cannot afford our publications.

I'm sure every one of you has thought about the doctoral student who walks across the stage, receives a diploma from you, shakes your hand, and then returns to Nepal, Kenya, or elsewhere. You say to yourself, "I wonder if this is the last time that this talented person will be able to read the newest publication in her specialty."

There are several ways one might think about the problem of the cost of scholarly publications. It is interesting how effective Internet2 became when a group of universities got together to drive it. We didn't look to an old organizational structure. We just did it.

I can't help but wonder what would happen if a number of universities set up a buying cooperative for publications. As part of the deal we would insist that the publications be made available on the Web to developing countries. Speaking as a lawyer, I believe you could work through the antitrust issues on this.

> Our U.S. funding agencies could simply require institutions receiving funds to place the resulting materials on the Web for developing countries.

The second thought is that U.S. funding agencies have a hammer here. What if they were to say that they no longer would pay page charges unless a publication were made available to developing countries, as well as to certain institutions in our own country, such as tribal colleges and historically Black universities?

You could go even further. Our U.S. funding agencies—I don't have a good grasp of the situation in Europe and Japan, but I think the problems have a familiar ring—could say, "Look, we're not going to allow your faculty to give away intellectual property rights," or they could simply require institutions receiving funds to place the resulting materials on the Web for developing countries.

What Harold Varmus did at the National Institutes of Health with BIOSCI was extremely interesting. By setting up electronic news groups and bulletin boards for biological scientists around the world, free of charge, BIOSCI pushed the issue of affordable publications.

I'm not suggesting there are any perfect solutions. But we haven't even had a good discussion of the enormous impact of the high cost of scholarly publications on developing countries.

If we are truly serious about closing the knowledge gap—and I know we all are—we must strengthen universities in developing countries and allow them to have, at affordable cost, the latest information that is produced in the rest of the world.

The knowledge gap issue carries some political dynamite. I served in Washington, D.C., for many years, and my sense is that we could accomplish something if we could tie the effort to some domestic constituencies. I could see U.S. Secretary of State Colin Powell taking positions on this issue and making them part of a G-7 or G-8 communiqué. In recent years, those communiqués have begun to broaden their subject areas. I suggest that's something to look at.

As each of us considers what international activities our campuses will enter into, particularly with developing countries, we should try to undertake them more than incrementally. Incrementalism is a good way to do things generally, but it seems to me that in some cases we need to jump start a process with something spectacular.

Incrementalism is a good way to do things generally, but it seems to me that in some cases we need to jump start a process with something spectacular.

Michigan State University is one of the most internationally oriented public universities in the United States. We have a very large number of international faculty and long experience using AID money to build universities on three continents. But when I came to the university nearly eight years ago I said, "If we're going to make another big leap, we've got to figure out something to drive it, something that will push everybody along." We settled on a much-expanded study abroad program. In this last year, we sent abroad 2,000 students. That's up from about 700 eight years ago. We've made a commitment that 40 percent of our graduates will study abroad. We are a big public university, with 43,000 students and a huge undergraduate program.

My point is that this commitment to study abroad is such a big deal, and we've pounded away at it so relentlessly, that it is beginning to have an impact on campus well beyond study abroad. I would suggest that other institutions could do the same—as many of you have.

Ladies and gentlemen, I'm intrigued, as I'm sure you are, with how we can close the knowledge gap between developed and developing countries. Thank you.

DISCUSSION

MR. GILLIS: I don't think anyone here doubts that study abroad is a transforming experience for most of our undergraduates. I might mention something we're doing at Rice University that's complementary to what MIT is doing. We're trying to help change the way people use the Web for education. We have a project called "Rice Connections," an open-source, Web-based system for modular, interactive learning, with annotated text. It is free to all comers. You don't have to stand in line. Just as with MIT, you just partake.

STEWART SUTHERLAND, Principal, University of Edinburgh in Scotland: I'd like to pick up the point in Peter McPherson's address about publications. We in the United Kingdom, and in the Russell Group of research universities, have been trying to move this issue forward, partly for altruistic reasons, but also for self-interested reasons.

We believe we are being systematically ripped off by a number of publishers. We buy back our own intellectual property at prices that increase much faster than the rate of inflation because one or two major publishers have cornered the market on high-quality publications in certain research areas.

We have set up a working group of university presidents and senior librarians that is looking into strategies. Just by setting up such a working group, we are sending a warning shot to the publishers that we cannot go on like this.

I put it to you. This might be the chance for us to put together an international group on this issue. If so, we are now in a position to put forward to AAU one or two names of people from the United Kingdom who could be part of a group to sit down and talk through how we all could use our intellectual property most efficiently, effectively, and, in view of today's discussion, most altruistically. I put a challenge to you.

MR. MC PHERSON: I'm all for it. I think it makes sense. I do believe that most countries have institutions that, by any measure, aren't able to buy the information but need it. So it is a domestic as well as an international issue.

Just as we cannot withhold key drugs from people because of market forces, we cannot keep knowledge out of the way. I think some collaboration makes sense, although AAU can best speak to this institutionally.

MR. GAEHTGENS: I think you need an international initiative. Most of the big publishing houses—and the two that you are thinking of—are truly international. If you start with the Russell Group that's fine, but you need to take the rest of the world along. Therefore I think it is a very good initiative.

MR. GILLIS: You could probably sign up half a regiment from the people in this room.

NILS HASSELMO, President, AAU: AAU currently is discussing a project on scholarly publication in collaboration with the Association of Research Libraries. We welcome contacts from you concerning possible international collaboration in that area.

GEORGE BABINIOTIS, Rector, the University of Athens: Regarding the Bologna Declaration, Professor Gaehtgens, what about reducing the years of undergraduate study from four to three years? We all speak about quality in universities. Do you think such a change can be positive, or will it make things worse?

MR. GAEHTGENS: As you are well aware, the discussion in Europe is very controversial because it cannot be conducted only at the level of university education. Both the secondary educational system and the characteristics of the labor market would be affected by changes in higher education. In addition, it makes a big difference whether the young people in your country graduate from high school at the age of seventeen or nineteen, whether you provide a college system, or whether graduates go directly from high school to the university. Therefore, a uniform answer satisfying all European countries is not likely.

> Globally speaking, university education in Europe does take too long—certainly in my country. Graduating from the university at age twenty-seven is too late.

In my country, many universities will not accept the reduction that you described. They argue that the three-year bachelor curriculum with only one major discipline would represent a significant loss of academic content, intellectual challenge, and what in German we call *bildung*. So there is no general agreement on this principle throughout Europe.

Globally speaking, university education in Europe does take too long—certainly in my country. Graduating from the university at age twenty-seven is too late. If we want to be internationally competitive, we must do something about it. In Germany, I would support a bachelor's degree curriculum of three years. However, there is nothing wrong with nations seeking different solutions to this issue, as long as university credits can still be generally transferred.

SABIH TANSAL, Rector, Bogazici University, Istanbul: With the implementation of summer school, many of our best students are finishing college in three years. Finishing in three-and-a-half years is not uncommon. These students are just as good as any—many receive fellowships at leading American universities. So four years is not required as long as there are appropriate, credit-based programs. If a good student can handle a little overload and take courses in the summer, three or three-and-a-half years is quite doable.

MR. GAEHTGENS: I totally agree.

PIOTR WEGLENSKI, Rector, Warsaw University: In my opinion, the Erasmus student exchange program in Europe is extremely important. Under this program, between 100 and 200 students each year from my university are able to attend universities in Western Europe.

But most student exchange in Europe comes from interuniversity exchanges. We have a network of such collaborations. At my university, there are four schools of law run in cooperation with French, German, British, and American universities. We also have an international master's of business administration program. Many universities in Poland are following the same path.

The underdeveloped world has widened significantly in recent years, with the addition of countries that formerly belonged to the Soviet Union. We heard last night from His Highness the Aga Khan about his university-building efforts in Kazakhstan, Pakistan, and Uzbekistan. The same also is

> The Erasmus student exchange program in Europe is extremely important, but most student exchange in Europe comes from interuniversity exchanges.

necessary for the more western parts of the former Soviet Union: White Russia, the Ukraine, and Moldavia. Education is a big reason why Russia is in very poor shape.

Poland, which is not in great economic shape but is much better off than the Ukraine or White Russia, is trying to build a university for the Ukraine and is organizing student exchanges. Actually, these are not exactly exchanges: they are unidirectional, with students coming to Poland from the Ukraine, White Russia, Lithuania, and Moldavia. We expect soon also to have students from the Balkans because of the economic and political situation in Yugoslavia. So I would draw your attention to this area of Europe where your help and cooperation are also needed. Thank you.

7

SUMMARY

AND

IMPLICATIONS

APRIL 23, 2001

In the last formal part of the program, we will give two of our colleagues an opportunity to ruminate on what has happened during the meeting, summarize what we have done, and comment on its implications.

Our two commentators will be George Rupp and Bernard Shapiro.

George Rupp was appointed president of Columbia University in 1993. At Columbia he has focused on enhancing undergraduate education and increasing the international orientation of the university. He came to Columbia from the presidency of Rice University and previously served as the John Lord O'Bryan Professor of Divinity and dean of the Harvard Divinity School. He spent extended periods studying and conducting research in Europe and Asia.

—Charles M. Vest
President, Massachusetts
Institute of Technology

Cultivating the Monastic and Scholastic Impulses of Our Universities

George Rupp
President, Columbia University

E HAVE BEEN TREATED TO KEYNOTE ADDRESSES AND FOUR PLENARY sessions that together posed a host of questions about our role as internationally oriented research universities in the twenty-first century. I will not attempt to summarize the wealth of detail provided in those sessions.

One way to see patterns in what we have been discussing is to look for them from the perspective of greater distance. Two of our colleagues have done that. Shigehiko Hasumi talked about the three generations of research universities. Alan Gilbert talked about faith-based versus secular universities, with the Enlightenment as the breakpoint between those two.

In reflecting on those two roughly chronological ways of providing a taxonomy, or typology, of the evolution of our universities, it occurs to me that neither goes back far enough.

The secular orientation of our universities, in fact, significantly antedates the Enlightenment in the West, while the second generation of research universities did not actually begin with industrialization and the utilitarianism that accompanied it. They came, instead, with the origins of the university in the modern West—in the Middle Ages. I'm going to take the risk of being thought to be nostalgic or indulging in utopian otherworldliness to take us a step farther back than those two typologies. It is a way of getting greater perspective on our discussions.

I apologize for going back in time only in the West. Other centers of higher learning existed before those of the western Middle Ages—in China, India, and the Mediterranean world. But the issues that we face as research universities arguably do originate in distinctions evident in the very beginnings of Western universities in the Middle Ages. So, if you'll indulge me, I will say a few words about another typological contrast—the contrast between "monastic schools" and "scholastic universities." I know that many of you will assume that neither of these institutions has anything to do with us and our preoccupations in these meetings, but, in fact, they go right to the heart of what we have been talking about.

The monastic school developed in the tenth or eleventh century for the spiritual formation of monks. For our purposes, its importance is that it was not designed to lead to any advantage in this world. It is also important to note that it was probably the most important educational institution from the tenth to the twelfth century in the West.

By the twelfth century, another kind of institution developed—the scholastic university, or *universitas*. The purpose of the scholastic university was secular, to prepare people for secular responsibility. This was true not only for those trained in theology, who—in contrast to monks—also had secular responsibilities, but also initially in law and medicine.

The earliest of those universities were in Paris and Bologna. In Paris, the students paid teachers fees in exchange for their instruction; in Bologna, teachers were actually hired and fired by their students.

As people traveled around Europe, it became clear that scholastic universities needed to adopt an element from the monastic schools. Although my account is highly simplified, that adoption proved to be the origin of what we now think of as residential colleges. By the mid-thirteenth century, the first of them—the Sorbonne in France and Oxford in England—had been founded, both named after the donors who gave money for them—another continuity with today.

In the monastic impulse, we can see the seeds of liberal education, curiosity-driven research, and pure scholarship not focused on immediate practical ends. In the scholastic impulse, we see responsiveness to social challenges, students as consumers, employers seeking skills, and government trying to promote competitiveness.

The pushes and pulls between these two impulses have been evident throughout our discussion. It's not surprising that the scholastic university, which evolved as secular and utilitarian, has been represented very strongly. The surprise is how vigorously the monastic impulse has been voiced by a broad range of people. One way to summarize what we have been talking about is to see how the two impulses have been reflected in our discussions.

The pattern began with the first plenary on globalization, economic development, and cultural identity. Not surprisingly, the scholastic university, the utilitarian secular university, is very evident here. The university must play a role in teaching skills needed by society.

Zhihong Xu very nicely showed how, in the People's Republic of China, that imperative places a special premium on recruiting individuals back to China who have been studying abroad. Henry Rosovsky talked about the fact that higher education has never been more important as a social creation, not only in the developed world but also in the developing world. The same theme was reiterated again and again during the meeting.

Speakers across the range of topics expressed the monastic impulse. The role of the university as the curator for the cultural equivalent of biodiversity was mentioned in session after session. Language, history, art, culture, and, particularly, local traditions must be cultivated so that we can resist homogenization in the midst of globalization. As Luis Alfredo Riveros said, it is important that we take responsibility for local and national cultural traditions.

> Language, history, art, culture, and, particularly, local traditions must be cultivated so that we can resist homogenization in the midst of globalization.

What I'm calling the monastic impulse was especially evident in the repeated expressions of skepticism about the marketplace. The message was that we need to recognize a public interest that is not reducible to the calculations of private profit through market mechanisms. A related challenge was that we adapt forms of liberal and general education appropriate for new circumstances and locations. Such education, we believe, is not a luxury for the developed world, but an important way to prepare leaders in both developed and developing nations.

Similarly, in research, the emphasis was on collaboration that develops an orientation to discovery and appropriate application, rather than simply importing technologies wholesale.

In the second plenary Robert Berdahl, Alec Broers, Juan Ramón de la Fuente, and Shigehiko Hasumi repeatedly emphasized the limits of the market and the need to support the arts and humanities, as well as science and technology.

In the third plenary, on the impact of information technology, Alan Gilbert and James Duderstadt showed themselves at home in the secular, utilitarian, scholastic university. Of all our speakers, Jim Duderstadt seems most at home there. Yet even Jim said we need to return to core values and basic questions as we steer our way through the revolutionary currents swirling around us.

Conversely, Nan Keohane placed her emphasis on the enduring value of liberal education and curiosity-driven, mentor-guided Ph.D. programs. Her presentation could be characterized in my typology as an expression of the monastic impulse. But she, too, recognized that the university must adapt to change.

Finally, in the fourth plenary Peter Gaehtgens talked about the importance not only of global competitiveness—the scholastic impulse—but also of the need to preserve regional traditions.

We heard from Peter McPherson of Michigan State University, an institution that has done a great deal to create socially useful knowledge both in this country and abroad. In that sense, his institution exemplifies what I've called the scholastic university. But Peter called our attention to the major initiative in study abroad at Michigan State. That massive program is very unusual at a public institution. The university took that step because studying in a very different place is a valuable way to shape the values, orientation, and sensitivity of our students.

So, from the tremendous range of our deliberations, I will hazard a summary lesson, which in effect repeats and summarizes what I've said

Of course we must continue to address the challenges of twenty-first century societies—economic competitiveness and globalization and all that they entail. We must continue our role in preparing professionals. We must work to deploy intellectual property to tackle social goals, including ones that address the needs of developing nations. We must serve society in a host of ways, from agricultural extension through Internet-assisted outreach. We must work at the kind of international collaboration that can be an antidote to unrestrained competitiveness.

But we also must remain faithful to our core purposes of liberal education and pure scholarship—curiosity-driven research—so as to attain a longer historical and a broader cross-cultural perspective. This stance is in deliberate tension with every provincial totaling up of the present attainments of a single country. This critical role, which universities historically have played, is an outgrowth of what I've called the monastic impulse. It resists the attempt to domesticate the university completely into its secular, utilitarian purposes.

Thank you very much.

Bernard Shapiro is principal and vice-chancellor of McGill University, his alma mater. After earning his doctorate in education from Harvard University, Dr. Shapiro began a career on the faculty at Boston University in the School of Education that has since taken him to administrative positions at Boston University, the University of Western Ontario, University of Toronto, and finally to McGill University, where he became principal and vice-chancellor in 1994.

Dr. Shapiro is the author of numerous articles on curriculum, public policy, and education, the development of logical thinking in young people, and educational research and methodology.

Balancing Old
and New Demands
on Universities

Bernard Shapiro

PRINCIPAL, McGILL UNIVERSITY

G EORGE AND I AGREED THAT WE WOULDN'T TRY TO SUMMARIZE THE meeting. Since we prepared independently, we were glad to learn when we compared notes a few minutes ago that we had quite different ways of responding to the presentations and discussion. I appreciated both the opportunity to make this presentation this afternoon—since it does make one listen more carefully during the day—and the opportunity to participate in this particular international meeting. We heard a range of voices that would otherwise not be present at AAU meetings. It was a valuable experience for me; I hope it was for the rest of the audience, as well.

We didn't hear many new things. There were no big surprises. But the opportunity to think about issues in a slightly more relaxed and stimulating way has been the value of the meeting.

The first issue that came up this morning focused on universities' efforts to balance complex competing demands. This has always been the case for universities. We have always been institutions that deal with complicated, often mutually contradictory demands on our priority system. What is different today are three relatively new factors that are making the balancing act more difficult.

One factor is globalization, which I prefer to think of as "re-globalization." Think back to the middle of the nineteenth century, when borders were opened by the invention of the telegraph. The past 150 years have been characterized by the closing down of that system. Now we are experiencing, in a much more complex and elaborate way, the reopening of our environment.

A second factor is, of course, information technologies. I won't pursue that any further.

The third factor, on which we have not focused, but which is equally important, is the changing structure of knowledge. If we cannot face that, none of the other elements will make much difference to anybody. The changing structure of knowledge is closely connected not only to globalization, but also to the vastly increased demand for postsecondary education.

The three factors have introduced some very difficult balancing acts, three of which are particularly problematic.

One is the need to be cooperative and competitive at the same time. We are not very good at bringing that off. Cooperation has long-term benefits, while competition has short-term payoffs. How are we going to balance those two things?

Another challenge is to balance being open and global—which leads to the kind of homogenization that one sees in shopping malls in the large cities of Asia, North America, and Europe—against the obvious need to preserve what was referred to this morning as "intercultural competence and experience." Although it is not clear that those two things can happen simultaneously, we would like them to.

English is fabulous as an international language. We all benefit from it, especially those of us for whom it is the mother tongue. But there is a whole other world out there.

On the other hand, because I live in Quebec, the notion of a meeting in which only English is spoken seems unnatural. English is fabulous as an international language. We all benefit from it, especially those of us for whom it is the mother tongue. But there is a whole other world out there. If this balance is going to be maintained—rather than abandoned to a new imperialism—one has to imagine that future meetings of this sort will be conducted in more than one language.

The third balancing act is the question of a civil society. I view this as a shorthand phrase for all of the issues that came up relative to the humanities, social sciences, and the arts. There is a balancing act between the needs of a civil society— which in North America is probably our largest single competitive advantage—and more immediate needs that don't relate, at least in the short term, to the question of a civil society. If we don't maintain this last balance, the other things will become more or less irrelevant.

> As I was growing up inside the university system, I became socialized to think—without ever having thought about it carefully— that the biggest threat to our autonomy was the government. It turns out, in retrospect, that government was the guarantor of our autonomy.

There is a series of ironies in our conversations here. I want to mention three. One is that as I was growing up inside the university system, I became socialized to think—without ever having thought about it carefully—that the biggest threat to our autonomy was the government. It turns out, in retrospect, that government was the guarantor of our autonomy because it believed we were important enough to preserve.

It is unclear how we will deal with what was referred to this morning as the persistence of nationalism coupled with the decline in the relative power of the nation-state. We are going to have to rethink our relationship to governments.

A second irony is differentiation among higher education institutions. We have long been accustomed to telling each other, at least inside the North American system and perhaps everywhere else, that differentiation is the price of mass higher education. Otherwise, the great research institutions, of which we like to think we are a subset, would have no opportunity to emerge.

But in listening to the conversation here yesterday and today, that differentiation also seems to have taken on another meaning, a differentiation as to place.

It might well be that what is appropriate in our experience is not appropriate in the experience of others. Developing countries will have a different development path and a different way of dealing with these problems, depending on the resources and ideas that are available to them.

The constant refrain is that the new access to information has made institutions less important and individuals more important. The reverse might actually be true.

We must be careful to avoid a new kind of imperialism. That is, as we talk about how we are going to close the knowledge gap—which is certainly worth addressing—we must not do so in such a way that we sustain the gap as a means of protecting the future of our own institutions.

Finally, there is what might turn out to be the irony of democratization. The constant refrain is that the new access to information has made institutions less important and individuals more important. The reverse might actually be true. Access to information is not the same as the capacity to deal with it in a productive way. Turning information into knowledge is the critical factor. We cannot assume that the mere availability of information will promote the democratization of higher education.

We have been talking about consortia—combinations of institutions to do this, that, or the next thing. Our interest in bigness might well turn out to yield another kind of irony. I happen to believe that big is often bad. The notion of a great blueprint in the sky to which we are all going to aspire and develop is just a way to explain away failure rather than to celebrate success. So how we manage collaborations in ways that makes sense to the institutions involved remains an unresolved question.

To close, I want to talk about three areas that I thought were underrepresented in the conversation of the past day-and-a-half.

The first is what we can do without imagining a dramatic new system. What are we doing, for example, about the composition of our student bodies? How many of us have a deliberate policy, say, of recruiting 20 percent of our students from other nations? That's just one example. How international is our faculty? It is not enough for us in North America to assume that because our faculty come from North America, they are up to international challenges. These are political issues, not just university issues, but there are things we can do to address them.

What are we doing about our fee structure? Are we going to continue to soak the foreign student while repeating that internationalization is what we're all about? What are we going to do about our own programs? What is the experience of students at any one of our institutions? How should our programs change to help our students become more effective adults in a more interdependent, international environment?

As our colleague, Derek Bok, former president of Harvard University, frequently says, higher education is not famous for understanding itself very well. Bok's statement remains an unanswered challenge.

The second issue, one that relates to what George Rupp described earlier about monastic and scholastic universities, involves the university as a social critic in this new environment. Social criticism is a crucial function of what we do, and we ought to think about it more clearly. As we become more collaborative and more involved in the environment around us, how are we going to keep sufficiently apart from it to enable ourselves to function effectively as social critics?

And, finally, something completely absent from the conversation was how research universities in this new environment relate to other knowledge-rich enterprises. There are many knowledge-rich enterprises out there. The question of how we relate to them in an effective and productive way seems to me worth a lot of consideration.

Some modesty is appropriate here. Earlier, we had a discussion about elementary and secondary education, a subject in which I have a personal interest. Someone wondered why, since it needed to be fixed, we didn't fix it. I cannot imagine a group more unable to fix elementary and secondary education than this one: not because we don't know enough—we know more than enough to be helpful—but because we have the wrong attitude. We are not willing to deal with the social problems that underlie its deficiencies. We are only willing to insist on setting the standards. There ought to be a more appropriate outcome, because down that road is a dead end.

We ought to be a bit modest about our roles in reforming elementary and secondary education and producing economic development. We don't want to oversell that issue. Many things we do don't lead to economic development, and many things done by other institutions do lead to it.

A little modesty will take us a long way, both as we deal with other knowledge-rich enterprises and with broad social problems.

The challenge remains. How do we help create graduates who are more intellectually and morally autonomous than they were when they first came to us? If we rise to at least some of the challenges that we propose to each other, we will be able to develop what has often been referred to as the "new republic of the intellect." Thank you.

DISCUSSION

MR. VEST: Thank you very much, George and Bernard, for those quite insightful comments. George Rupp left me with a very deep philosophical point to ponder. As he characterized my good friend, Jim Duderstadt, I suddenly realized that the only president who spoke at this meeting who is clearly at home in the new digital age is the only one who is no longer in office.

Are there any last questions or comments that anyone wishes to make or any inquiries of our two summarizers?

STEWART SUTHERLAND, Principal, University of Edinburgh in Scotland: I was very utilitarian earlier in the afternoon. Now I'd like to be more high-flown and idealistic.

Words that have been associated with universities but that we haven't spoken much today are "knowledge," "truth," and "values."

These three words are still important. I want to tie them up with an emphasis on the humanities and the arts. I am a humanist. That's my trade. I am used to being told by engineers, physicists, and chemists—now digitally several times a day—what the real truth is. It is rather nice just occasionally to hear artistic, humanistic people being lauded in some way.

It is confession time. Many of us in the humanities, the arts, and, to some extent, the social sciences, have let the side down a bit by not insisting that words like knowledge, truth, and values be central to discussion somewhere in the university. We have tried to ape the specialists who have been so successful in the sciences and the technologies.

I urge myself, as I urge you, to talk with deans of arts, humanities, and social sciences. Ask them if they raise the big questions about where something leads in terms of truth, knowledge, and values. Ask if they insist on knowing what is important about a given activity.

I offer a plea to keep these questions on the agenda, to force those of us in the humanities back to seeing them as part of our responsibility.

MR VEST: If there are no other comments or questions, thank you all for a wonderful day.

8

THE VIEW FROM THE U.S. STATE DEPARTMENT

APRIL 23, 2001

INTRODUCTION

Charles M. Vest
PRESIDENT
MASSACHUSETTS INSTITUTE OF TECHNOLOGY

I CAN'T THINK OF ANY AUDIENCE THAT WOULD SYMPATHIZE MORE WITH MY assignment here tonight. Surely it's an experience that unites university presidents everywhere: five or ten times a year, you're asked to introduce someone who, as the saying goes, needs no introduction.

Our guest tonight has achieved that level of accomplishment and celebrity—not only in the United States but also around the world.

We know about his recent appointment as this country's secretary of state, about his exemplary leadership as chairman of the U.S. Joint Chiefs of Staff, and about the talent and perseverance that eventually earned him the rank of four-star general.

Many of us also know about the deliberate detour he took, at the close of his Army career, to lead an organization called "America's Promise," an organization designed to rekindle the American commitment to volunteer service of every kind.

Many of us also probably have some sense that he has lived a quintessentially American story—what he has called his "American journey"—

starting out as the son of immigrants from Jamaica in a hardscrabble corner of the South Bronx, and winding up in the most exalted corridors of power.

Despite everything we already know about Secretary of State Colin Powell, it's exciting to be able to introduce him to this particular audience—because in a surprising sense, he's working for us.

You might think that managing America's foreign policy and running the State Department would be enough responsibility for anyone. But he also has appointed himself a round-the-clock, round-the-globe ambassador for the transforming power of education.

He is a product of the New York City public schools and the fabled City College of New York. He portrays education—not just in terms of schooling, but in terms of study and curiosity and relentless self-improvement—as the story of his life. He has made it his personal mission to spark that passion for education in young people everywhere on earth.

As leaders of institutions of higher learning in America and around the world, we could not ask for a better ally.

My friends, allow me to introduce Secretary of State Colin Powell.

EDUCATING
TOMORROW'S
LEADERS

Colin L. Powell
UNITED STATES SECRETARY OF STATE

T
HANK YOU, CHAIRMAN VEST, FOR THAT VERY KIND INTRODUCTION.
I am pleased to be here among so many of America's and the world's
most prestigious leaders in the field of education. I welcome the
opportunity to speak to so many talented people gathered together to discuss
the many challenges and competing interests that vie for our attention each
week in this globalizing, fast-paced world.

I often use the metaphor of the kaleidoscope to describe today's world.
We all remember when we were kids and we would turn that marvelous little tube to the light and watch the crystals coalesce and separate and coalesce
again, forming beautiful new patterns. Our world is like that today—and I'm
certain the patterns that form and re-form for you at your universities are
every bit as challenging as those that confront a secretary of state.

In meeting those challenges, I want you to know that you have a powerful ally in America's president. One of his top priorities is education.
President Bush understands how crucial it is to get education right. If a

nation does not have an educated workforce, an educated electorate, an educated people, that nation will soon be lost in the demanding world of today and tomorrow.

Such education calls for a system that starts at the elementary and secondary levels, where the all-important, brick-and-mortar foundation is laid. In that respect, we know we have a challenge ahead of us in America. We have to improve our elementary and secondary education system. And while we do it, we have to be sure we leave no child behind.

> We have to reach out as well to the youngsters in our society who are not so privileged, not so able to step up to our collective tables and partake of the educational banquet we offer to them.

We cannot just reach out to the elite, to the well off, to the young people we know will succeed, important though this is. We have to reach out as well to the youngsters in our society who are not so privileged, not so able to step up to our collective tables and partake of the educational banquet we offer to them.

Before returning to government, I was chairman of a group called America's Promise—The Alliance for Youth. The mission of America's Promise is to help create five crucial conditions in every disadvantaged child's life: a healthy start, a safe place, a caring adult, a marketable skill, and a chance to give back, to render service to the community.

In our efforts to create these conditions, some of the most important partners we recruited to help us were universities and colleges. We called them universities and colleges of promise. I got the idea in 1998 when I met with the president of the University of Southern California, Steven Sample. President Sample is here tonight I believe.

Howard University was easy to recruit to our alliance. I was on the board. I was also chairman of Howard's Academic Excellence Committee. And the university system in Minnesota put every campus in the state into its concept of a university of promise. I am grateful to President Mark Yudof for that overwhelming response.

At the end of the day, we must ensure that our educational systems from bottom to top embrace all of our children because we will need every one of our citizens in the challenging decades ahead. So our countries must reach out to each other and share and exchange ideas and students and best practices.

In this respect, the American Association of Community Colleges has some exceptionally effective programs. With funding from the U.S. Agency for International Development, this group promotes partnerships between community colleges in America and institutions of higher learning in other countries.

A two-year branch of Kent State University, for example, is working with Tashkent State University in Uzbekistan to provide education in environmental technology. Columbus State Community College in Ohio is partnered with the Dar es Salaam Institute of Technology in Tanzania to create an information technology institute.

There are other ways to share and to partner for wider and better education. During the 1999–2000 academic year, for example, America hosted more than half a million foreign students in its colleges and universities. And I know everyone in this audience is familiar with America's flagship exchange effort, the Fulbright Program. Both America and the host countries contribute to this program. It is without doubt the finest example of educational excellence in America's scholarship kitbag. A quarter of a million people have benefited from a Fulbright experience since the program began fifty-five years ago.

A very small sampling of the program's alumni includes Brazil's president Fernando Cardoso, Intel chief executive officer Craig Barrett, writer Eudora Welty, opera star Renee Fleming, AAU president Nils Hasselmo, and Ruth Simmons, Brown University's incoming president. In addition, more than twenty Fulbright alumni are Nobel laureates.

> The Fulbright Program is without doubt the finest example of educational excellence in America's scholarship kitbag. A quarter of a million people have benefited from a Fulbright experience since the program began fifty-five years ago.

Such programs as these provide opportunities for intellectual and personal growth each year to thousands of American and international scholars, students, teachers, and professionals.

They also encourage and sustain democratic practices, build mutual understanding, create a cohort of future leaders who understand each other's countries from the inside, and promote long-term linkages between institutions here and abroad.

Such cooperation ultimately strengthens democracy and the bonds between nations. And these "people to people" programs have taken on increased significance in the globalized, interdependent, information-based world in which we live.

The U.S. government does not have a monopoly on such programs. Nor do we have the requisite wisdom to determine all the future exchange programs that may be essential to building a better, more educated world. That's why we need to proceed in strategic partnership with you. Together, we need to develop programs that can meet the multiple needs of nations, their peoples, and their institutions. And one of the most pressing needs is for engineers, scientists, and computer specialists.

The National Research Council produced an excellent report for the State Department in 1999. One of its conclusions was that thirteen of the sixteen stated objectives of American foreign policy encompassed science, technology, or health considerations.

So it is very critical that we place the proper emphasis on science and technology, on mathematics, and on the other skills and fields of knowledge that contribute so decisively to shaping this transforming world.

In the United States, we recognize that we are not producing enough graduates in science and engineering to fill the needs of our scientific and technological communities. That's why we have to borrow so many from overseas.

> We are not producing enough graduates in science and engineering to fill the needs of our scientific and technological communities. That's why we have to borrow so many from overseas. Without them, the prolonged economic success we've had for over a decade would have been impossible.

I want to thank all of you here who have had a hand in educating some of these wonderful people, because without them, the prolonged economic success we've had for over a decade would have been impossible.

But we have to do more within our own educational structure to make up for this deficit. A great example of how to do this is the International Science and Engineering Fair.

More than a million students in grades nine through twelve from all over the world compete in regional science fairs. More than 1,200 of these young people from more than forty different countries earn the chance to compete for $3 million in scholarships and prizes. For the past five years, Intel Corporation has added its prestige and money to the sponsorship and support of this exciting event.

This science and engineering fair is a superb way to collaborate internationally, and it's an excellent example of nonprofit and corporate partnership as well.

Most of you will likely have scouts at this international fair, looking over the scene for prospective students. If you don't have such a reconnaissance planned, you should.

Science doesn't have a country. It doesn't have any borders. Science today gets around with the speed of light.

Science doesn't have a country. It doesn't have any borders. Science today gets around with the speed of light. Indeed, most knowledge is just a click away. And the fact that knowledge moves with the speed of light means a very different context in which to educate—a very exciting, thrilling, and dramatically changed context.

I know that all of you are dealing with that change right now, trying to maximize this ongoing revolution for your purposes of education and collaboration. Whether it's distance learning, webcasting to multiple audiences, exchanging data, or simply conducting research, the Internet has opened up new possibilities—possibilities that all of you are on the cutting edge of discovering, exploiting, and turning into educational progress and advantage.

This is important work because your public and private institutions are the principal source of the fundamental knowledge that drives, nourishes, and constantly refreshes the innovation and technology of our Information Age.

Your institutions are also playing an important role in foreign policy. One of the president's fundamental goals is to build constructive relationships with other nations that will contribute to achieving a peaceful and prosperous world. In seeking to create closer ties among the world's great universities through events such as tonight's dinner, you are building those relationships. Moreover, there are many challenges of a global nature that are common to all of our countries—the oceans, weather and climate, infectious diseases, natural disasters, and nonproliferation of weapons of mass destruction.

These challenges are becoming major elements of the world's foreign policy agenda. Since your institutions are the basic source of the new knowledge that must be drawn upon to address them, you are intimately involved in this additional aspect of foreign policy. So I am pleased that you have chosen to come to the State Department this evening.

This event will be a stunning success if all of you leave this building with an even greater sense of the importance of your work in educating tomorrow's leaders—the leaders who will eventually build the peaceful and prosperous world that we all look forward to. Go forth from here and deliver this vital message to educators the world over.

APPENDIX 1
BIOGRAPHIES OF SPEAKERS

Charles M. Vest is president of the Massachusetts Institute of Technology. After earning a B.S. degree in mechanical engineering at West Virginia University, he earned M.S.E. and Ph.D. degrees at the University of Michigan, where he joined the faculty in 1968. He then served as the university's dean of engineering, vice president for academic affairs, and provost before assuming the presidency in 1990. Dr. Vest is a fellow of the American Association for the Advancement of Science and a member of the National Academy of Engineering. He serves on the board of directors of IBM and the E.I. du Pont de Nemours & Company. He is chairman of the Association of American Universities.

Globalization, Economic Development, and Cultural Identity: Forces and Counterforces

Henry Rosovsky is Lewis P. and Linda L. Geyser University Professor, emeritus, at Harvard University. After receiving his B.A. degree from the College of William and Mary, he earned his M.A. and Ph.D. degrees at Harvard University. Thereafter, he was a professor of economics and history, and chair of the Center of Japanese and Korean Studies, at the University of California, Berkeley. In 1965 Dr. Rosovsky returned to Harvard, where he later became chairman of the economics department and associate director of the university's East Asian Research Center. From 1973 to 1984 he served as dean of the Faculty of Arts and Sciences, where he supervised a major reorganization of Harvard's undergraduate curriculum. He was acting president of the university in 1984 and 1987. He has written extensively on economic development, particularly in Japan and Asia. His books include *The University: An Owner's Manual.* He is a fellow of the American Academy of Arts and Sciences and received the Clark Kerr Medal for service to higher education from the University of California, Berkeley. The French government made him a *chevalier* of the Legion of Honor in 1984, and in 1988 he received the Order of the Sacred Treasure (Star) from the Japanese government. In 2000 he co-chaired a task force on higher education, convened by the World Bank and UNESCO. The task force published its results under the title *Higher Education in Developing Countries: Peril and Promise.*

Zhihong Xu is president of Peking University. After earning a master's degree in botany from the Shanghai Institute of Plant Physiology of the Chinese Academy of Sciences in 1969, Professor Xu took on and retains the positions of vice-president of the Chinese Academy of Sciences, vice-chair of the China's national committee for UNESCO, vice-chair of the Chinese Society of Biotechnology, chair of the Chinese Society of Cell Biology, and vice-chair of the Chinese Society of Botany. He became president of Peking University in December 2000. He has published more than 150 papers, reviews, and reports in plant development, plant biotechnology, and plant tissue and cell culture.

Luis Alfredo Riveros is rector of the University of Chile. Dr. Riveros earned his master's and doctoral degrees in economics from the University of Chile and the University of California, Berkeley. He is professor of economics at the University of Chile and has served as chair of the department of economics and the graduate school of economics, as well as dean of the school of economics and business administration. In 1998 he was elected to a five-year term as rector of the university, Chile's oldest and largest. As a professional economist, he has been an economic adviser to several Latin American governments and organizations and consulted for the World Bank, the Inter-American Development Bank, and the U.S. Agency for International Development. He has lectured and written extensively on labor economics and economic development and has published three books, including *Lectures in Econometrics.* He is director of Chile's Asia-Pacific Foundation and the former director of the Latin American Association of Business

Schools. His recent work has concentrated on educational issues, particularly the management and financing of higher education.

Shared Issues in International Higher Education

His Highness the Aga Khan is the forty-ninth hereditary Imam of the Shia Imami Ismaili Muslims, a community that resides in some twenty-five countries, mainly in West, Central, and South Asia; Eastern Africa and the Middle East; and North America and Western Europe. He emphasizes that Islam is a thinking, spiritual faith—one that teaches compassion and tolerance and upholds the dignity of man. In consonance with that view he has established and leads several private, international, nondenominational development agencies collectively known as the Aga Khan Development Network.

Two of those agencies are active in higher education. The first is the Aga Khan University, established in 1983 as the first private university in Pakistan. The university has concentrated on research and professional education in the fields of nursing, medicine, and education. Future plans include an undergraduate college of arts and sciences in Karachi, a program in advanced nursing studies in East Africa, and an institute of Islamic civilizations in London.

The second is the Aga Khan Trust for Culture, which supports programs and activities designed to enrich the training of professionals in architecture and related fields with reference to the Islamic world. In addition to the endowed Aga Khan Programme for Islamic Architecture at Harvard and MIT, the Trust is working with MIT's School of Planning and Architecture to create a global, Web-based resource for students, teachers, scholars, and professionals in the field of architecture.

Last year, the Aga Khan launched another initiative in higher education when he signed an international treaty with the presidents of Tajikistan, Kyrgyzstan, and Kazakhstan to create the University of Central Asia. The new university will be the first in the world devoted exclusively to research and training on the problems and potentials of mountain peoples and the settings in which they live. The Aga Khan is chancellor of the Aga Khan University and chancellor-designate of the University of Central Asia.

Competing Demands on Universities

Robert M. Berdahl is chancellor of the University of California, Berkeley. After earning his Ph.D. from the University of Minnesota in 1965, Dr. Berdahl became a member of the history faculty at the University of Oregon and later served five years as dean of the university's college of arts and sciences. In 1986 he became vice-chancellor for academic affairs at the University of Illinois at Urbana-Champaign, where he served until 1993, when he assumed the presidency of the University of Texas at Austin. In 1997 he became chancellor of the University of California, Berkeley. He has served as a research fellow at the Institute of Advanced Study at Princeton and the Max Planck Institute for History in Göttingen, Germany, and has written extensively on German history. He is vice-chair of the Association of American Universities.

Alec N. Broers is vice-chancellor of the University of Cambridge. He obtained a B.Sc. degree in physics and electronics at Melbourne University, and B.A., Ph.D., and Sc.D. degrees in electrical engineering at Cambridge. After spending nearly twenty years working for IBM in the United States, he returned to Cambridge University in 1984, where he was elected professor of electrical engineering and fellow of Trinity College (1985) and, subsequently, master of Churchill College and head of the university engineering department. He has served on numerous committees of NATO, the British government, and the European Economic Community and has received a number of awards and prizes, including the American Institute of Physics Prize for Industrial Applications of Science. He is a fellow of the Royal Society, the Royal Academy of Engineering, the Institute of Electrical Engineers, and the Institute of Physics, and a foreign associate of the U.S. National Academy of Engineering. He was knighted in 1998.

Juan Ramón de la Fuente is rector of the National Autonomous University of Mexico. After earning his medical degree from the university, he continued postgraduate training in psychiatry at the Mayo Clinic in Rochester, Minnesota. At the National Autonomous University of Mexico, where he still is a professor of psychiatry, he served as director of clinical research, vice-chancellor of science, and dean of the medical school. He then was appointed secretary of health for Mexico, where he launched a major reform of the nation's health care system. In 1999, he returned to his alma mater to become rector. Dr. De la Fuente has published more than 250 papers and 13 books, and has lectured around the world. He was vice-president of the World Health Assembly in Geneva, chaired the UNAIDS program, and is a member of the board of directors of the International Association of Universities. He was president of the Mexican Academy of Sciences, and is president-elect of the National Academy of Medicine in Mexico.

Shigehiko Hasumi is the former president of the University of Tokyo. After completing his undergraduate and master's degrees in French literature at the University of Tokyo, he studied at the University of Paris on a French government scholarship, where he received his doctorate in French literature in 1965. Following his appointment to the faculty at the university in 1973, he was the dean of the faculty of arts and sciences from 1993 to 1995, before becoming vice-president of the university. He became president in April 1997 and served through March 2001. His books cover diverse areas in literature and film criticism. In 1978, he received the Yomimuri literature prize for *Against the Japanese Language*. A prominent film critic, he has served on the juries of several international film festivals. Dr. Hasumi's honors include the French government's highest award for art and culture, the Commandeur des Arts et Lettres, which he received in 1999.

The Impact of Information Technology on Universities

Alan D. Gilbert is vice-chancellor of the University of Melbourne. After earning a doctor of philosophy degree in modern history from the University of Oxford in 1973, Professor Gilbert taught history at universities in Australia and Papua New Guinea before becoming pro-vice-chancellor of the University of New South Wales in 1988, and then vice-chancellor of the University of Tasmania in 1991. He became vice-chancellor of the University of Melbourne in 1996. Widely published in British and Australian history, he was joint general editor of an eleven-volume history of Australia commissioned to celebrate the nation's bicentenary in 1988. He is a fellow of the

Australian Academy of the Social Sciences and chair of Universitas 21, an international association of research-intensive universities.

James J. Duderstadt is president emeritus of the University of Michigan. After taking his Ph.D. in engineering science and physics from the California Institute of Technology in 1967, he joined the engineering faculty at the University of Michigan, rising to dean of engineering in 1981 and provost and vice-president for academic affairs in 1986. Appointed president of the university in 1988, he served until 1996. He now holds a university-wide faculty appointment as University Professor of Science and Engineering. A recipient of the U.S. National Medal of Technology, Dr. Duderstadt is also a member of the National Academy of Engineering, the American Academy of Arts and Sciences, and Phi Beta Kappa. He chairs major national study commissions in federal research policy, higher education, information technology, and nuclear energy.

Nannerl O. Keohane is president of Duke University. After earning her Ph.D. from Yale University in 1967, she taught at Swarthmore College, the University of Pennsylvania, and Stanford University before assuming the presidency of Wellesley College in 1981. She became president of Duke University in 1993. Dr. Keohane holds the rank of professor of political science and has written extensively on political philosophy, feminism, and education. She is a fellow of the American Academy of Arts and Sciences and a member of the Council on Foreign Relations. She serves on the boards of IBM, the Colonial Williamsburg Foundation, and the Research Triangle Foundation of North Carolina, among others. She is a member of the executive committee of the Association of American Universities.

Trends in International University Collaboration

Malcolm Gillis is Ervin Kenneth Zingler Professor of Economics and president of Rice University. After earning his Ph.D. at the University of Illinois, he taught economics at Duke and Harvard universities. Later, at Duke, he served as dean of the graduate school, vice provost of academic affairs, and dean of the faculty of arts and sciences. He assumed the presidency of Rice

University in 1993. His research and teaching have focused on the national and international issues of fiscal reform and environmental policy. Among his many publications is the leading textbook in its field, *Economics of Development*. He is a director of the Federal Reserve Bank of Dallas, the Council for Higher Education Accreditation, and the Business–Higher Education Forum. He also is a founding director of International University Bremen in Germany.

Peter Gaehtgens is president of the Free University of Berlin. After earning a medical degree from the University of Cologne in 1964, he went on to become a university lecturer, assistant professor, and professor there. In 1967–69, Professor Gaehtgens was a research fellow at the California Institute of Technology. In 1983 he was appointed professor at the Institute of Physiology at the Free University of Berlin and became the institute's director in 1987. He went on to serve as vice-president of the medical departments of the university, and then as dean of the Department of Human Medicine. In 1997 he became vice-president and acting deputy to the president. Two years later he became president. He is a full member of the Berlin-Brandenburg Academy of Sciences.

M. Peter McPherson is president of Michigan State University. After earning an MBA from Western Michigan University and a law degree from American University, he served in several agencies of the U.S. government, including the White House, where he was special assistant to President Gerald Ford. He then served as both chairman of the board of the Overseas Private Investment Corporation and administrator of the U.S. Agency for International Development from 1981 to 1987. He left AID to become deputy secretary of the U.S. Department of Treasury and then joined the Bank of America, where he managed global debt restructuring and the bank's work in Latin America and Canada. He became president of Michigan State University in 1993. He is a member of the board of Dow Jones, Komatsu, and the American Council on Education. He has received the U.S. secretary of state's Distinguished Leadership Award and the U.S. Presidential Certificate of Outstanding Achievement. UNICEF honored him for his outstanding contribution to child survival.

Summary and Implications

George Rupp is president of Columbia University. After receiving a bachelor's degree from Princeton University and a bachelor's of divinity degree from Yale University, he earned his Ph.D. at Harvard University. He spent long periods studying and conducting research in Europe and Asia. Before becoming president of Columbia in 1993, Dr. Rupp served as John Lord O'Brien Professor of Divinity and dean of the Harvard Divinity School and spent eight years as president of Rice University in Houston, Texas. He is the author of four books, including *Beyond Existentialism and Zen: Religion in a Pluralistic World*.

Bernard J. Shapiro is principal and vice-chancellor of McGill University. After earning his doctorate in education from Harvard University in 1967, he joined the faculty of Boston University and later became associate dean of the institution's school of education. He returned to his native Canada in 1976 to become dean of the faculty of education at the University of Western Ontario in London, Ontario. Two years later he was appointed academic vice-president and provost of the university. After serving in various public service positions, including deputy minister of education for the province of Ontario, he joined the University of Toronto in 1992 as a professor of education and public policy. In 1994, he became principal and vice-chancellor of McGill University. Dr. Shapiro was appointed officer of the Order of Canada in 1999. He also is past president of the Canadian Society of Education and of the Social Science Federation of Canada. He is the author of numerous articles on curriculum, public policy in education, and educational research and methodology.

The View from the U.S. State Department

Colin L. Powell is secretary of state of the United States of America. After earning a bachelor's degree in geology at the City College of New York in 1958, he was commissioned in the U.S. Army as a second lieutenant. He later earned an MBA at George Washington University. In the Army he rose to the rank of four-star general and served as chairman of the Joint Chiefs of Staff, the highest military position in the Department of Defense. In 1991 he oversaw Operation Desert Storm in the Persian Gulf. Following his retirement from the Army, Secretary Powell wrote a best-selling autobiography, *My American Journey*, and became a popular public speaker. He chaired America's Promise—The Alliance for Youth, a national nonprofit organization focused on young people. He was sworn in as secretary of state in January 2001. A two-time recipient of the Presidential Medal of Freedom, Secretary Powell has also earned the President's Citizens Medal, the Congressional Gold Medal, and the Secretary of State Distinguished Service Medal. He holds honorary degrees from universities and colleges around the country.

APPENDIX 2
PRESIDENTS AND CHANCELLORS OF AAU MEMBER INSTITUTIONS APRIL 2001

Jehuda Reinharz   Brandeis University
Sheila E. Blumstein   Brown University
David Baltimore   California Institute of Technology
Jared L. Cohon   Carnegie Mellon University
David H. Auston   Case Western Reserve University
David M. O'Connell   The Catholic University of America
George Rupp   Columbia University
Hunter R. Rawlings III   Cornell University
Nannerl O. Keohane   Duke University
William M. Chace   Emory University
Neil L. Rudenstine   Harvard University
Myles Brand   Indiana University
Richard Seagrave   Iowa State University
William R. Brody   The Johns Hopkins University
Charles M. Vest   Massachusetts Institute of Technology
Bernard J. Shapiro   McGill University
M. Peter McPherson   Michigan State University
L. Jay Oliva   New York University
Henry S. Bienen   Northwestern University
William E. Kirwan   The Ohio State University
Graham B. Spanier   The Pennsylvania State University
Harold T. Shapiro   Princeton University

Martin C. Jischke	Purdue University
Malcolm Gillis	Rice University
Francis L. Lawrence	Rutgers, The State University of New Jersey
John L. Hennessy	Stanford University
Kenneth A. Shaw	Syracuse University
Scott S. Cowen	Tulane University
William R. Greiner	University at Buffalo– State University of New York
Peter Likins	University of Arizona
Robert M. Berdahl	University of California, Berkeley
Larry N. Vanderhoef	University of California, Davis
Ralph J. Cicerone	University of California, Irvine
Albert Carnesale	University of California, Los Angeles
Robert C. Dynes	University of California, San Diego
Henry T. Yang	University of California, Santa Barbara
Don Michael Randel	University of Chicago
Elizabeth Hoffman	University of Colorado System
Charles E. Young	University of Florida
James J. Stukel	University of Illinois, Urbana-Champaign
Mary Sue Coleman	University of Iowa
Robert E. Hemenway	University of Kansas
Dan Mote	University of Maryland, College Park
Lee C. Bollinger	University of Michigan
Mark G. Yudof	University of Minnesota, Twin Cities
Richard L. Wallace	University of Missouri, Columbia
L. Dennis Smith	University of Nebraska, Lincoln
James C. Moeser	University of North Carolina at Chapel Hill
David B. Frohnmayer	University of Oregon
Judith Rodin	University of Pennsylvania
Mark A. Nordenberg	University of Pittsburgh
Thomas H. Jackson	University of Rochester
Steven B. Sample	University of Southern California
Larry R. Faulkner	University of Texas at Austin
Robert J. Birgeneau	University of Toronto

John T. Casteen III	University of Virginia
Richard L. McCormick	University of Washington
John D. Wiley	University of Wisconsin-Madison
Gordon Gee	Vanderbilt University
Mark Wrighton	Washington University in St. Louis
Richard C. Levin	Yale University
Nils Hasselmo	Association of American Universities

Appendix 3
International University
Leaders Participating in the
Convocation

John D. Gerhart
President
American University in Cairo
Egypt

John Waterbury
President
American University of Beirut
Lebanon

Sabih Tansal
Rector
Bogazici University
Turkey

André J. Oosterlinck
Rector-President
Catholic University of Leuven
Belgium

Ivan Wilhelm
Rector
Charles University in Prague
Czech Republic

Arthur Kwok-cheung Li
Vice-Chancellor
The Chinese University of Hong Kong
Hong Kong

Tatchai Sumitra
President
Chulalongkorn University
Thailand

Brazão Mazula
Rector
Eduardo Mondlane University
Mozambique

Peter Gaehtgens
President
Free University of Berlin
Germany

Menachem Magidor
President
The Hebrew University of Jerusalem
Israel

Kari Raivio
Rector
Helsinki University
Finland

Jürgen Mlynek
President
Humboldt University of Berlin
Germany

Makoto Nagao
President
Kyoto University
Japan

Gabriel de Nomazy
President
École Polytechnique
France

Douwe D. Breimer
Rector Magnificus
Leiden University
The Netherlands

Jean-Yves Mérindol
President
Louis Pasteur University of Strasbourg
France

Andreas Heldrich
Rector
Ludwig Maximilian University, Munich
Germany

George Babiniotis
Rector
National and Kapodistrian University of
Athens
Greece

Juan Ramón de la Fuente
Rector
National Autonomous University
of Mexico
Mexico

Wei-Jao Chen
President
National Taiwan University
Taiwan

Choon Fong Shih
Vice-Chancellor
National University of Singapore
Singapore

Tadamitsu Kishimoto
President
Osaka University
Japan

Zhihong Xu
President
Peking University
China

Ki-Jun Lee
President
Seoul National University
Korea

Sheng-wu Xie
President
Shanghai Jiao Tong University
China

Carlos Angulo-Galvis
Rector
University of the Andes
Colombia

Marija Bogdanovi
Rector
University of Belgrade
Yugoslavia

Alec N. Broers
Vice-Chancellor
University of Cambridge
United Kingdom

Luis Alfredo Riveros
Rector
University of Chile
Chile

Kjeld Møllgård
Rector
University of Copenhagen
Denmark

Gabriel Macaya
Rector
University of Costa Rica
Costa Rica

Matthew Laban Luhanga
Vice-Chancellor
University of Dar Es Salaam
Tanzania

Stewart Sutherland
Principal
University of Edinburgh
Scotland, United Kingdom

Asman Boedisantoso R.
Rector
University of Indonesia
Indonesia

Alan D. Gilbert
Vice-Chancellor
University of Melbourne
Australia

Anuar Zaini Md. Zain
Vice-Chancellor
University of Malaya
Malaysia

Kaare R. Norum
Rector
University of Oslo
Norway

Jacques Marcovitch
Rector
University of São Paulo
Brazil

Gavin Brown
Vice-Chancellor
University of Sydney
Australia

Shigehiko Hasumi
Former President
The University of Tokyo
Japan

Takeshi Sasaki
President
The University of Tokyo
Japan

Piotr Weglenski
Rector
University of Warsaw
Poland

Hans Weder
Rector
University of Zürich
Switzerland

Bo U. R. Sundqvist
Rector
Uppsala University
Sweden